Heirloom
Ribbonwork

Ribbon
Creations
for the Next
Generation

Helen Gibb

Published by

700 E. State St.
Iola, WI 54990-0001
Telephone 715-445-2214
www.krause.com

Please call or write for our free catalog. Our toll-free number to place an order or obtain a free catalog is 800-258-0929 or please use our regular business telephone 715-445-2214 for editorial comment and further information.

Photographer: Sara Frances,
Important Occasions Photography,
Denver, Colorado
Illustrator: Karen Wallach,
Denver, Colorado

Library of Congress Catalog
Number: 00-111289

ISBN: 0-87341-991-X

Printed in the United States of
America

A note about the cover photo:
Modern ribbon roses decorate a scarf chatelaine, while an antique German half doll pincushion, a sewing bird, an Edwardian sterling chatelaine, and a pin cube remind us of our needlework heritage - links that bind us together through the generations.

Dedication

To Mum and Dad -

with love and appreciation

for all you have given to me.

Rolled edge petals make the roses in this vintage composition. Collection of Deborah Piefke.

Lord and Taylor millinery and dry goods catalogue, circa 1890. Collection of the author.

A basket of vintage rosette flowers and leaf loops, with intriguing side compositions. Overall size is 16" by 4-1/2". Any guesses as to what it might have embellished? Was it part of a dress girdle, was it worn as a headband, was it stitched to a hat or...? Collection of Meron Reinger.

Credits

A book like this doesn't get written without the help and support from others. I would like to publicly say thank you to everyone who helped me, supported me, and encouraged me along this continuing ribbon journey. Bouquets and thanks are sent to all of you.

Thanks to all my ribbon students for experimenting with my designs. And special thanks to Liz, Mary Jo, Michelle, and Vicki for the extra support you have provided me over the years, and to Diana for upholstering the footstool.

Bouquets go to Edith Minne at Renaissance Ribbons who has provided me with exquisite French ribbons, continuous support, and cherished friendship. Merci, mon amie!

A big thank you to Diana Coit of Artemis, Inc. and Brooke Exley of Hanah Silk for all the lovely bias-cut silk ribbons used in many of the projects in the book.

And thanks to Mokuba ribbons for the exceptionally beautiful velvet ribbons used in the Tea Caddy project.

Gracious thanks to Beth Hill for making and painting the most beautiful reproduction porcelain half dolls in the world. Your work is exquisite!

Heartfelt thanks to: Meron Reinger and Deborah Piefke for the generous loan of their vintage ribbonwork pieces. Frieda Marion, and Marc and Shona Lorrin for writing the best books on antique half dolls and for answering my questions. I have been inspired! Mary Jane Hamilton and Phyllis Sarver for friendship and old lace!

Thanks to my photo shoot support team - Anita, Vicki, and Sonja. It couldn't have been done without you.

And many thanks to two very talented ladies who made the artistry of the book so beautiful: Sara for her wonderful photographs, and Karen for her lovely illustrations.

And thanks are in order for my editor Barbara Case who not only edited the text, but also waded through all my e-mails, answering lots of questions.

Kind thanks to the Colorado Historical Society for the use of the Grant Humphreys mansion.

Special thanks to The Metropolitan Museum of Art, Costume Institute for permission to use the Boue Souers dress photograph on page 68.

A special bouquet of thanks goes to my friend Kim who offered me respite from the "daily grind" in the form of glorious days of sunshine, blue skies, pine trees, and aspens at her mountain home. All she had to say to me was, "Bring the laptop." I went!

Thanks to my daughter, Melinda, for once again, being my model of choice. I love you!

And the book could not have been written without the support and love of my husband, Jim. Thank you!

Vintage ribbon flowers in a basket, on crinoline. Collection of Meron Reinger.

Table of Contents

Introduction .8

Before You Begin 11

Chapter 1

Boxes and Baskets 13

The Bride's Box 14

Blue Tea Caddy 16

Wooden Basket 19

Dresden Flowers 22

Chapter 2

Half Dolls Updated 24

Grace on a Vanity Box 25

Lady Madeline Pincushion 28

Clara Tassel 32

Lady Eleanor Lavender Sachet 34

Chapter 3

Brooches With Flair 37

Brown Brooch 38

Peach Brooch 41

Autumn Brooch 44

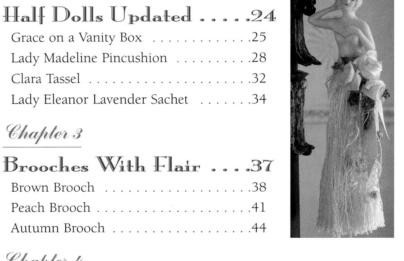

Chapter 4

Hats and More 46

Pink Hat With Rose 47

Purple Hat 50

Black Hat With Brown Rose
    and Feathers 52

Hat Needle Case/Pincushion . .54

Floral Hatpin Holder 57

Chapter 5

Ribbon Flower Embellishments 60

Red Purse 61

Scarf Chatelaine 64

Flowers for a Ball Gown 67

Chapter 6

Ribbonwork in Your Home . . 71

Moon Cottage Album 72
Footstool With Cabochon Roses 74
Lavender-Filled Sachet 76
Parasol With Flowers 79
Roses on the Wing 82

Chapter 7

Flowers to Grow 84

Spring Bulbs - Tulips, Jonquils, and Daffodils .85
Magnolias and Berries 92
Wild Rose Posy .94

Ribbon Techniques Guide . .96

Stamens .96
Twisting Ribbon 97
Knots 97
Shirring 97
Ruching 98
Pleating 99
Loops 100
Tubes 101
U-Gathers 103
Petals 108
Folded Rose 111
Leaves .113
Combination Rose Guide 118

About the Author 122
About the Grant Humphreys Mansion .123
Bibliography 124
Resources 125
Index 127

Ribbon roses, blossoms, and embroidered leaves cover the top of this circa 1900 French vanity box. Collection of the author.

Introduction

A French vanity box, circa 1900, with brushes, comb, powder puff, powder box, and beveled mirror. Each element is covered in ribbonwork, and the powder puff is topped with a porcelain "half doll related" rose. Collection of the author.

Heirloom Ribbonwork

*L*ittle did I know how wonderfully involved I would become in the world of ribbon when I wrote my first book, *The Secrets of Fashioning Ribbon Flowers*. Since that book I have been "exposed" to all sorts of exciting ribbon adventures, I have met some very knowledgeable ribbon experts, and have seen much in the way of vintage ribbonwork.

But the thing I have enjoyed the most in this creative world of ribbon is you - the reader of this book. I have enjoyed seeing you become interested in ribbonwork and I have loved seeing the ribbon flowers you've made. Because of this, and your insatiable desire to learn more about ribbonwork, I've been inspired to keep researching the old techniques so I can create new designs and present them to you. I heartily thank you for sharing your time, your resources, and your talents for the purpose of perpetuating ribbonwork. Ribbonwork may have been a lost art several years ago, but it isn't anymore. Let's all share what we know and pass it down to the next generation.

Sprinkled throughout the book are some vintage pieces of ribbonwork that I wanted to share with you. Two very generous collectors have loaned many of these pieces to me and some pieces are from my own collection. Most of the pieces are 1920's floral compositions created on crinoline and many of them were most likely used on clothing, cushions, and the like. Be inspired by the lovely ribbons and the floral designs. I was!

Also of note are the vintage ribbonwork books I have collected, which are shown on page 10. These books are our link to the past, for both ribbonwork and the dear little porcelain half dolls. The three 1920's books, titled *Ribbon Art*, are filled with a vast range of ideas for ribbon usage on girdles, boudoir items, hat trimmings, half dolls as pincushions (and telephone covers!), and ways to make flowers for lingerie. The smaller black book was one in a series of text books produced by the Woman's Institute of Domestic Arts and Sciences, Inc., in the mid 1920s to educate women students in the ways of trimming with ribbons and fabrics, embroidery, and other domestic arts and sciences. *The Ribbon Book* by Diamond Dyes is from the 1890s and tells women how they can change the look of their clothing by dying and reusing some of the ribbons. These volumes have been so wonderful to look at.

The projects in this book are quite diverse in their range, style, and complexity. There is truly something in here for everyone! My hope is that those who have begun their ribbon journey will continue with this delightful art form and my challenge to those who have not yet tried their hand at ribbonwork is to "give it a go," as we Aussies would say.

Homemade ribbon fancies. The ribbonwork uses two-toned silk satin ribbons and is for lingerie applications, circa 1925. Collection of the author.

A lovely basket of petal flowers mounted on cardboard, with the original label. French, circa 1920s. Collection of Meron Reinger.

Samples of vintage ribbon flowers fall from the pages of old ribbon books dating from the late 1890s through the 1920s.

I know it is tempting to just jump in and start a ribbon project, but I would encourage you to browse through the book and become familiar with its contents and layout first. One section that you should pay particular attention to is the **Ribbon Techniques Guide**, starting on page 96. You will be referred there many times throughout each project. This is the "nuts and bolts" of the book, as it explains how to make the bows, flowers, and leaves in a very easy to understand diagram format. Included in this section is the **Combination Rose Guide** (pages 118-121) - invaluable for recognizing the techniques used for many of the roses in the projects.

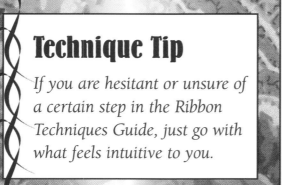

Technique Tip

If you are hesitant or unsure of a certain step in the Ribbon Techniques Guide, just go with what feels intuitive to you.

Supplies

Before you start a project, read over the supply list and gather the items needed. It is assumed that you will have scissors, needles and thread, and the other basics, so these items are not listed on the project supply list.

The following is a basic list of ribbon-work supplies that are handy to have. In addition to a stash of ribbons, trims, lace, beads, buttons, stamens, and other embellishing "do-dads" you will need:

* **sharp scissors**
* **pointed embroidery scissors**
* **tape measure**
* **milliners needles** (size 10)
* **curved needle**
* white **beading thread** (size G 33)
* **crinoline**
* thread-covered **florist wire** in sizes 18, 20, 22, 30, and 32-gauge
* small **needle-nose wire cutters**
* green **florist tape**
* **tacky glue**
* **hot glue gun** and glue sticks (not used often but just in case)

Some ribbon tips:

* Buy at least a yard of any ribbon you are buying.
* Buy the best quality you can afford. There is a difference in ribbon quality, which you will discover after you have worked with the ribbons.
* Vary the colors you buy, remembering that you can't have too many greens.
* Choose all styles of ribbons - wire-edge, bias-cut silk, ruffled-edge, velvet, jacquards, grosgrain, and whatever else pleases you.
* Select a range of widths that include 1-1/2", 1", 5/8" wide, and narrower.

The First Stitch

Most ribbonwork is hand stitched. Use about 18" of thread and only a single thickness in your sewing. If you are in the habit of knotting your thread before you take that first stitch, I must caution you not to rely on a knot to hold the gathered ribbon. Train yourself to lock that thread in the ribbon by taking several backstitches (one stitch on top of another) before you begin any stitching. Secure your gathering the same way.

Regarding the stitch length - try what feels right. A general rule is that the smaller, or narrower the ribbon, the smaller the stitch should be. The opposite is true for the wider ribbons. Experiment!

What about the "G" word - glue? Traditional ribbonwork is always stitched. This means that the petals are stitched, the flower is assembled with stitches, and the compositions are all stitched to crinoline. Does this mean you can't use glue? No, it doesn't. In certain instances it's all right to use glue - tacky glue, or in some cases, hot glue. For example, you have to use tacky glue to secure ribbon to a solid surface - as in the Tea Caddy (page 16) and the Wooden Basket (page 19) or if you are finishing the back of a brooch with Ultrasuede. And sometimes I glue the petals of a large flower together if I know it is going to be used in a floral arrangement for my home. But I will not use glue if the item is something I'm going to wear or if it is something that I want to treasure over the years. You decide.

Chapter 1
Boxes and Baskets

The Bride's Box   *Page 14*

Blue Tea Caddy   *Page 16*

Wooden Basket   *Page 19*

Dresden Flowers   *Page 22*

The Bride's Box

Trimmed boxes were very popular items during the early 20th century. This new box has been decorated in vintage style silk prints and ribbon trims and is topped with exquisite ribbon roses and beaded ribbon leaves.

This charming nostalgic box is a very easy project to do. By simply gluing (yes, the "G" word!) some silk prints, ribbons, and trims to a pre-covered box (easily found in your local craft shop), you can have a wonderful box in no time. The tricky bit is the folded roses. Some of you will have no trouble with this rose but if this is your first time making it, you will want to practice beforehand. The finished box would make a lovely gift for a bride to store much of her wedding day memorabilia in.

You will need:

Oval box, fabric covered (7" w x 5-3/4" w x 6-1/2" h)
4 small silk prints - "Ladies" (approx. 4" x 3")
64" pink/green flower bud ribbon trim
48" beige double ruffled-edge ribbon, 3/4" wide
1 yd. off-white wire-edge ribbon, 1-1/2" wide
1 yd. ivory wire-edge ribbon 1-1/2" wide
1 yd. pale pink wire-edge ribbon, 1-1/2" wide
1 yd. blush pink wire-edge ribbon, 1-1/2" wide
1 yd. dusty pink wire-edge ribbon, 1-1/2" wide
18" green bias-cut silk ribbon, 1" wide
2 yds. olive green wire-edge ribbon, 1-1/2" wide
7" pink ruffled-edge ribbon, 1/4" wide
7" off-white ruffled-edge ribbon, 1/4" wide
7" dusty pink ruffled-edge ribbon, 1/4" wide
8" green ruffled-edge ribbon, 1/4" wide
60 clear seed beads
20 ivory or pearl beads
6 miniature pink dagger beads
2" square of crinoline
Glue stick
Tacky glue

Steps:

Apply the silk prints, ribbon, and trims to the box:
1. Cut each silk print in an oval shape. (*Tip:* Use a cardboard oval template about 3-1/2" by 2-1/2" purchased from your local craft/frame shop or make your own.) Use the glue stick to apply a light coating to the wrong side edges of each silk print and adhere two prints to each side of the box.
2. Without precutting the flower bud ribbon trim, apply tacky glue to the back of the trim and place it around the edges of each silk print. Start the glu-

ing/trimming in the area that will be covered by the miniature roses and beads (see photo). Cut the trim after you have edged around each oval. Seal the ends with glue or fabric sealer.
3. Glue the beige ruffled-edge ribbon around the base of the box and around the side of the lid.
4. Cut the remaining flower bud trim into 16 sections about 1" long. Seal the ends of the ribbon trim with glue or fabric sealer to prevent fraying. Evenly space and glue eight of the sections to the beige ribbon around the lid and eight to the beige ribbon around the box base.

Make the roses and leaves:
1. **Large roses**: Refer to diagrams 32a-32f (page 111) to make five large folded roses, using one yard of 1-1/2" wide ribbon for each rose (all colors except green). Glue these roses to the top of the box.
2. Refer to diagrams 7a-7b (page 98) to ruch 18" of bias-cut 1" wide green silk ribbon. Use 1-1/2" spacing for the ruching. Gather to the fullness needed to cover the raw edges of the roses.
3. **Small roses**: Refer to diagrams 18a-18c (page 103) to make six coiled roses, using 3-1/2" of 1/4" wide ruffled-edge ribbon for each (off-white, pink, dusty pink).
4. Cut two crinoline circles, 1" diameter, and stitch three small roses to the center of each, making a miniature rose composition.
5. **Prairie point leaves**: Refer to diagrams 35a-35d (page 113) to make 14 prairie point leaves, using 4" of 1-1/2" wide olive green wire-edge ribbon for each.
6. Sew a pearl bead to each leaf tip. Glue the leaves under the large roses so the raw edges of the leaf don't show.
7. **Half-boat leaves**: Refer to diagrams 38a-38e (page 116) to make four half-boat leaves, using 2" of 1/4" wide ruffled green ribbon for each. Trim the raw edges and stitch two leaves next to the miniature roses in each composition. Set aside the two compositions.
8. **Beading**: Refer to the beading guide below and make six bead dangles, three for each miniature rose composition.
9. Stitch each string of beads under the roses. Cut away the excess crinoline and glue one rose composition to the front of the box between the set of silk prints, and one on the back.

Clear seed beads

Ivory or pearl bead

Dagger bead

Blue Tea Caddy

The English wooden tea caddy, circa 1800, was the inspiration for creating this new velvet box tea caddy suitable for tea bags!

When you cover a plain square box with exquisite velvet ribbons and trims you will have made a very elegant tea caddy, suitable for presenting tea bags to your guests when you entertain. And if you have enough ribbon left over, you can make a velvet ribbon presentation pouch for your own personal tea bag when you are away from home. Tuck one of these single tea bag pouches inside a card as a little gift for someone special.

There's nothing like a good cup of tea. For as long as I can remember tea has always been an important part of my day and it seems that the kettle is always on for another "cuppa." Having tea is also a very social activity, whether you are hosting a tea party or having tea for two, and it can often be a great comfort to someone in need of a quiet chat with a trusted friend.

A favorite tea tradition for me is the early morning cup of tea, which is especially memorable when I go home to Australia to visit my family. Dad will bring us all an early morning cup of tea in bed. Before you can truly savor that first sip, someone will knock on your door, peek their head around, and come in with their cup of tea. Before you know it, we are all gathered in the bedroom - sitting on the end of the bed, lounging in the chair or on the floor - chattering away like little birds. This is when our day really starts - with family, love, and tea.

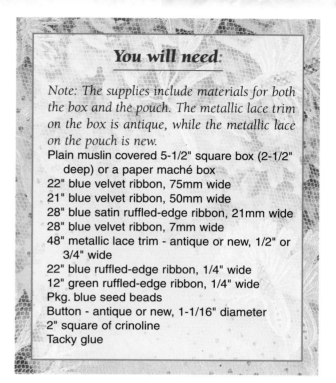

You will need:

Note: The supplies include materials for both the box and the pouch. The metallic lace trim on the box is antique, while the metallic lace on the pouch is new.

Plain muslin covered 5-1/2" square box (2-1/2" deep) or a paper maché box
22" blue velvet ribbon, 75mm wide
21" blue velvet ribbon, 50mm wide
28" blue satin ruffled-edge ribbon, 21mm wide
28" blue velvet ribbon, 7mm wide
48" metallic lace trim - antique or new, 1/2" or 3/4" wide
22" blue ruffled-edge ribbon, 1/4" wide
12" green ruffled-edge ribbon, 1/4" wide
Pkg. blue seed beads
Button - antique or new, 1-1/16" diameter
2" square of crinoline
Tacky glue

Steps:

Cover the box:
Refer to the photo for placement of all the ribbons.
1. Cut two 7" lengths of 75mm blue velvet ribbon. Lightly glue them to the top of the box and the side where the ribbon will overhang. Butt the ribbons together on top of the lid and smooth them over the top and sides.
2. Cut one 7" length of 21mm blue satin ruffled ribbon and lightly glue it to the center of the box lid, over the blue velvet ribbons.
3. Cut one 7" length of 7mm blue velvet ribbon and lightly glue it to the center of the satin ribbon.
4. Cut two 7" lengths of metallic lace trim and glue them on each side of the satin ribbon and just under the ruffles.
5. Cut four 2-1/2" lengths of metallic lace trim and glue each one to a corner.
6. Cut one 21" length of blue satin ruffled-edge ribbon and lightly glue it around the side of the box lid so all the raw edges of the metallic lace and velvet ribbon are covered. For a neater appearance, position all the seams in the back of the box.
7. Cut one 21" length of 7mm blue velvet ribbon and lightly glue it to the center of the blue satin ruffled-edge ribbon around the side of the box lid.

8. Glue the 21" length of 50mm blue velvet ribbon around the sides of the bottom of the box.

9. Glue the remaining metallic lace trim over the velvet at the base of the box bottom.

Make the ribbon and button medallion:

1. Glue the button to a 2" circle of crinoline. (You may have to cut off the shank for the button to lie flat.)

2. Refer to diagram 10 (page 99) to pleat the 1/4" wide blue ruffled-edge ribbon with 1/4" pleats. Pleat enough ribbon and test it around the button before cutting off the remaining ribbon.

3. Stitch the pleated ribbon to the crinoline just under the edge of the button.

4. Refer to diagrams 17a and 17c (page 103) to make 12 u-gather leaves from the 1/4" wide green ruffled-edge ribbon, using 1" for each. Place these evenly around and just under the blue pleated ribbon and stitch in place.

5. Stitch the blue seed beads around the button and on top of the blue pleated ribbon. Cut away any excess crinoline.

6. Attach the button medallion to the center of the box. This can be glued or stitched on with a curved needle.

Seed beads and narrow ribbons made into pleats and leaves encircle an antique French button.

Project Tip

My friend Vicki recommends painting the edges of the box with acrylic paint in a color to match the ribbons before adhering the ribbon to the sides. You'll find that any edge the ribbon does not quite cover will be visually filled in with the matching paint color.

Bonus Idea

Make a little tea bag pouch from the scraps of ribbon left from the Tea Caddy. Fold up a 7" piece of the 75mm velvet ribbon. Close the side seams with whip stitches. Make a pleated ruffle from the blue ribbon and sew it to the flap. Add some metallic lace, a ribbon rosette, and some beads.

Wooden Basket

A recycled wooden basket embellished with French jacquard ribbons and a lid decorated with ribbon roses and leaves.

Before becoming involved in ribbonwork I was a decorative painter and this small wooden oval basket is a leftover from those days. The wood is stained a light walnut color. The basket has solid wooden sides, a wooden handle, and originally, no lid. I made a fabric-covered cardboard lid and used a glass button to make a knob that rises about 1" above the thread-sculpted roses and leaves.

If you don't have a wooden basket, use any type of oval box/basket (paper maché, cardboard, etc.), even one that has a lid already on it. Adapt the supplies and the instructions to the type and size of box/basket you have. If you go this route, you will need to paint the box/basket in an attractive color before applying the ribbons.

You will need:

Oval wooden basket (or substitute) 6-1/2" l x
   4-3/4" w x 3" d
20" black/gold jacquard ribbon, 5/8" wide
20" black/gold jacquard ribbon, 1-3/4" wide
20" green/gold woven jacquard ribbon, 3/4"
   wide
48" gold wire-edge ribbon, 1" wide
12" flower bud ribbon trim
10" red picot-edge ribbon, 1/4" wide
10" green ruffled-edge ribbon, 1/4" wide
10" yellow/green ruffled-edge ribbon, 1/4"
   wide
20" green ruffled-gold-edge ribbon, 1/4" wide
4 gold seed beads
Crinoline oval, 4-1/2" x 4"
2 pieces cardboard, 7" x 6"
2 pieces 1/4" thick batting, 7" x 6"
2 pieces gold silk dupioni fabric, 8" x 7"
Gold silk dupioni fabric, 2" w x 4" l
4" of 22-gauge thread-covered wire
1" diameter glass button
Tacky glue
Hot glue
Wire cutters

Steps:

Decorate the basket:

1. Apply a light coat of tacky glue to the back of the 5/8" wide black/gold jacquard ribbon and glue it over the handle.

2. Repeat with the wider black/gold jacquard ribbon and the green/gold ribbon and glue them around the sides.

Make the flowers and leaves:

1. Roses: Refer to diagrams 32a-32f (page 111) to make four folded roses using 12" of the gold wire-edge ribbon per rose. Trim the excess ribbon from the stems.

2. Red rosettes: Refer to diagrams 17a and 17d (page 103) to make four red rosettes using 2-1/4" of 1/4" wide red picot-edge ribbon for each rosette. Cover the center with one gold seed bead.

3. Half-boat leaves: Refer to diagrams 38a-38e (page 116) to make four half-boat leaves. Use 2-1/4" of green ruffled ribbon for each. Make four more from the yellow/green ruffled ribbon and eight more from the green gold-edge ribbon. Set aside four gold-edge leaves. Divide the remaining leaves into four groups, with one of each color leaf in each group. Set aside the four groups.

Put the composition together on crinoline:

A small composition of thread-sculpted folded roses, rosettes, and leaves.

Refer to the photo for the placement of the elements.

1. Stitch the roses to the crinoline oval, leaving a 1-1/16" uncovered oval in the center of the crinoline.
2. Refer to diagrams 34a-34b (page 112) to thread-sculpt the roses into shape. After the roses are stitched, cut away the crinoline that is exposed in the center. (This hole is where the button knob will be.)
3. Between each rose stitch a group of three leaves in a fan shape.
4. Make four small circles with 3" of the flower bud ribbon trim. Stitch one circle on top of each leaf group. The flower bud ribbon trim will overhang the hole in the middle of the crinoline so just turn it under and stitch it to the back of the crinoline.
5. Stitch a red rosette in the center of the flower bud circle.
6. Cut away the excess crinoline. Set the composition aside until after the lid is made.

Make the button knob:

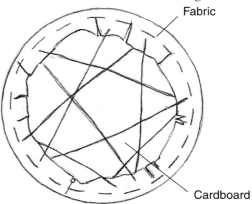

1. Thread 4" of wire through the button shank and twist the wire.
2. Cover the wire stem by folding the small 2" x 4" strip of silk fabric so its width measures about 1" and roll it around the wire stem. Turn under the raw edges at the end of the fabric and glue the roll closed. Put a dab of glue on the fabric edge that touches the button and push the rolled fabric up tight against the button.
3. Stitch four gold-edge leaves around the silk fabric stem. Set aside.

Make the lid:
1. Trace the top opening of the box/basket onto both pieces of cardboard and cut out the shapes.
2. Glue a piece of batting to each of the cardboard ovals and trim the excess.
3. Use scissors and reduce the size of one of the cardboard ovals by 3/8" all the way around.
4. Using each of the cardboard templates as a guide and adding 1" margins all around, cut the two pieces of silk fabric.
5. Stitch around the edge of the fabric ovals, leaving a 1/4" margin.
6. Place the larger of the fabric pieces over the batting on the largest cardboard oval, tighten the gath-

ering, and secure with stitches on the back of the oval. Repeat this step for the small piece of fabric and the small cardboard oval.
7. Attach the button knob by using an awl to pierce a small hole in the center of the largest fabric covered oval. Dab some glue on the bottom edge of the fabric on the button knob and push the wires through the hole until the fabric stem is flush with the lid. On the back of the cardboard, bend the stem wires flat and secure with a dab of hot glue.

Fabric

Cardboard

8. Quickly hot glue the wrong side of the small fabric oval over the wrong side of the large fabric oval. The wires are now sandwiched between the cardboard ovals that make up the lid.

Top of lid

Bottom of lid

9. Place the ribbon flower composition over the button knob and adhere it to the lid with stitches or a little dab of glue.

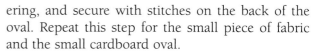

Project Tip

For neat seams, fold the raw edges of the ribbon back before overlapping and gluing to the basket.

Dresden Flowers

Use a variety of different ribbon rose styles and blossoms in your compositions.

Use your imagination for displaying these exquisite ribbon flowers. The wire basket is simply inspiration for you. Embellish a cushion, a wedding photo album, or simply frame this beautiful composition of ribbon flowers. Make a smaller arrangement of flowers from left over ribbons that can be worn as a brooch.

You will need:

36" off-white ruffled-edge satin ribbon, 21mm
21" pink ruffled-edge sheer ribbon, 20mm
13-1/2" off-white picot-edge sheer ribbon, 25mm
11-1/4" pale pink wire-edge grosgrain ribbon,
   1" wide
6" taupe satin-edge sheer ribbon, 15mm
12" variegated sheer pink gold-edge organdy
   ribbon, 1/2" wide
22-1/2" lavender bias-cut silk ribbon, 7/16" wide
11-1/4" ruffled-gold-edged mauve ribbon, 1/4"
   wide
12" dark green picot-edge sheer ribbon, 25mm
12" pink/green wire-edge ribbon, 1-1/2" wide
10" pale green wire-edge grosgrain ribbon, 1"
   wide
3 pale green velvet millinery leaves
3 pale taupe satin millinery leaves
5 long purple/green single-head stamens
4 pink/green double-head stamen buds
30 mauve seed beads
7" square of white crinoline

Steps:

Make the flowers and leaves:

1. Pink/off-white double folded rose: Refer to the folded rose diagrams 32a-32f (page 111) to make one rose. Use 10" of 21mm off-white ruffled-edge satin and 10" of 20mm pink ruffled-edge sheer ribbon together.

2. Large off-white combination rose: Refer to Rose #10 in the Combination Rose Guide (page 120). Use 7" of 21mm off-white ruffled-edge satin for the folded rose center. Use 2-1/2" of 25mm off-white picot-edge ribbon for each of the three single u-gather petals for the middle petals. Use 12-1/2" of 21mm off-white ruffled-edge satin for the five-petal u-gather outer petals. This is a cabochon rose with petals. Stitch the folded rose center to a 3/4" circle of crinoline. Stitch the three petals around the folded rose center. Stitch the u-gather petals under the cabochon rose.

3. Small off-white combination rose: Refer to Rose #5 in the Combination Rose Guide (page 119). Use 6" of 21mm off-white ruffled-edge satin for the folded rose center. Use 6" of 25mm off-white picot-edge sheer for the four-petal u-gather outer petals. Wrap and stitch the u-gather petals around the folded rose center.

4. Pale pink/taupe combination rose: Refer to Rose #8 in the Combination Rose Guide (page 119). Use 6" of taupe sheer for the folded rose center. Use 2-1/4" of 1" wide pale pink wire-edge grosgrain for each of the five rolled corner outer petals. Evenly arrange and stitch the five rolled corner petals around the folded rose center. Trim the excess ribbon at the base.

5. Pink cabochon rosebuds: Refer to Rose #2b in the Combination Rose Guide (page 118) to make two cabochon rosebuds. Use 6" of 1/2" wide variegated sheer pink gold-edge organdy for each of the folded rose centers. Use 2-1/2" of 20mm pink ruffled-edge sheer ribbon for each of the three single u-gather outer petals. The folded rose is stitched to a 1/2" circle of crinoline. Stitch the single u-gather petals in place over the folded rose center and under the crinoline.

6. Lavender loop blossoms: Refer to diagram 15 (page 100) to make three loop blossoms. Each blossom has six loop petals. Use 1-1/4" of lavender ribbon for each loop. Secure the petals around one purple stamen.

7. Mauve rosettes: Refer to diagrams 17a and 17d (page 103) to make five rosettes, using 2-1/4" of 1/4" wide mauve ribbon for each. Cover the center of each with six mauve seed beads.

8. Mitered leaves: Refer to diagrams 39a-39d (page 117) to make four mitered leaves. Use 3" of the 25mm wide dark green sheer ribbon for each leaf.

9. Boat leaves: Refer to diagrams 37a-37e (page 115) to make two boat leaves. Use 5" of 1" wide pale green wire-edge ribbon for each leaf.

10. Prairie point leaves: Refer to diagrams 35a-35d (page 113) to make three prairie point leaves. Use 4" of 1-1/2" wide pink/green ribbon for each.

Put the composition together on crinoline:

1. Working from the back of the composition forward and referring to the photo, stitch the leaves and flowers to the crinoline. Begin with the velvet leaves, add the ribbon leaves, double-folded rose, large off-white rose, pale pink/taupe rose, small off-white rose, and two pink rosebuds. Tuck in more small leaves, three lavender loop blossoms and purple stamens, five mauve rosettes, and a small bunch of pink/green stamen buds.

2. Trim the crinoline and stitch the composition to the base you have decided on for display.

Chapter 2
Half Dolls Updated

Grace on a Vanity Box   Page 25

Lady Madeline Pincushion   Page 28

Clara Tassel   Page 32

Lady Eleanor Lavender Sachet   Page 34

Grace on a Vanity Box

Ribbon flowers and pre-made ribbon trim decorate this half doll vanity box.

Boxes were very popular bases for half dolls in the 1920s. They often contained powder and sat on a lady's dresser or were sometimes given as candy boxes. Some were quite elaborate while others were on a simpler scale.

The oval box shown was purchased covered with plain muslin and had a padded top. You too can turn a plain box into something exquisite just by covering your box with silk fabric, ribbons, trims, and a half doll. If you choose to use another size or shape of box, remember to adjust the quantities and measurements of materials in the instructions.

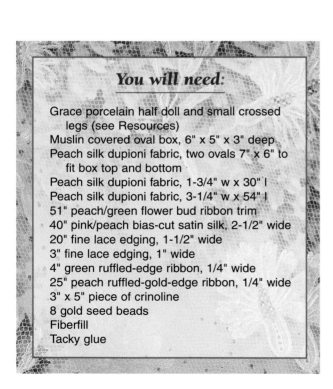

You will need:

Grace porcelain half doll and small crossed legs (see Resources)
Muslin covered oval box, 6" x 5" x 3" deep
Peach silk dupioni fabric, two ovals 7" x 6" to fit box top and bottom
Peach silk dupioni fabric, 1-3/4" w x 30" l
Peach silk dupioni fabric, 3-1/4" w x 54" l
51" peach/green flower bud ribbon trim
40" pink/peach bias-cut satin silk, 2-1/2" wide
20" fine lace edging, 1-1/2" wide
3" fine lace edging, 1" wide
4" green ruffled-edge ribbon, 1/4" wide
25" peach ruffled-gold-edge ribbon, 1/4" wide
3" x 5" piece of crinoline
8 gold seed beads
Fiberfill
Tacky glue

Steps:

Cover the box:

1. Lid top and underside of box: Lightly glue the edges of the box lid and the lid sides with tacky glue. Apply one of the peach fabric ovals to the top of the lid, smoothing out the fabric. Do the same for the underside of the box.

2. Side of lid: Turn under and press the long edges of the 30" of 1-3/4" piece of peach fabric so the finished width of the fabric measures 1". Refer to diagram 5 (page 97). Gather the fabric. Glue along the gathering stitches and fit the fabric around the lid side.

3. Side of box: Turn under and press the long edges of the 54" x 3-1/4" piece of peach fabric so the finished width of the fabric measures 2-1/2". Refer to diagram 5 (page 97). Gather the fabric. Glue along the gathering stitches and fit the fabric around the box side.

4. Glue enough flower bud ribbon trim to decorate the top edge of the lid and the bottom edge of the box. You will have 11" of trim remaining.

Make the rosettes and leaves:

1. Peach rosettes: Refer to diagrams 17a and 17d (page 103) to make eight rosettes, using 2-1/2" of peach ruffled-gold-edge ribbon for each. Cover the centers with one small gold seed bead. Seven of the rosettes will go around the half doll's dress and one will go in the composition for the front of the box.

2. Leaves: Refer to diagrams 38a-38e (page 116) to make two half-boat leaves, using 2" of green ruffled-edge ribbon for each leaf.

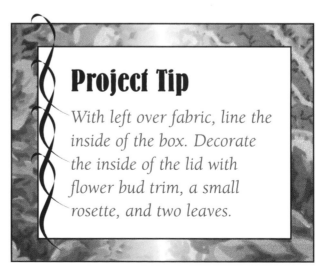

Project Tip

With left over fabric, line the inside of the box. Decorate the inside of the lid with flower bud trim, a small rosette, and two leaves.

Make the half doll's dress:

1. Cut a 2-1/2" circle of crinoline. Gather 20" of 1-1/2" wide lace edging to fit around the crinoline circle and stitch it to the edge.

2. Refer to diagrams 21a-21c (page 104) to make five rose petals, using 5-1/2" of pink/peach bias-cut silk ribbon for each petal. Fold the ribbon in half so the width of the ribbon is reduced to 1-1/4" and press flat. Sew the petals to the crinoline in a circle, leaving 3/4" at the center.

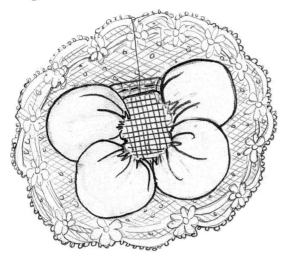

3. Sew the half doll to the center of the petal circle. Sew seven peach rosettes around her waist to cover the sew holes and the join between the half doll and the petals.

Make the half doll's cushion and attach the legs:

1. Refer to diagram 16a-16b (page 101) to make a tube from 10" of the pink/peach bias-cut silk ribbon. Gather the top edge tightly. Turn the ribbon tube inside out.

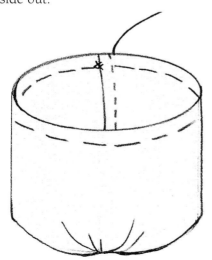

2. Fill the cavity with fiberfill, then gather the bottom edge tightly. Flatten the stuffed tube (think flat tomato or berry) and secure the shape with stitches.

3. Sew 8" of flower bud trim around the widest circumference of the cushion.

4. Sew the porcelain legs to the front of the flat cushion.

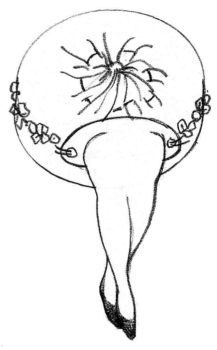

5. Cover the legs with 3" of the peach gold-edge ribbon where they join the cushion.

6. Place the half doll on the cushion, align the half doll to the legs, and stitch together.

7. With a curved needle, sew the half doll/cushion to the top of the box

Make the rosette decoration for the box:

1. Tightly gather the 3" length of narrow lace edging. Stitch this to a 1" circle of crinoline.

2. Referring to the picture for placement, stitch the ribbon rosette, flower bud trim, and two leaves over the lace.

3. Trim the excess crinoline and attach the composition to the box front with glue or stitches.

Lady Madeline Pincushion

Surrounded with new and vintage ribbonwork, this new half doll pincushion evokes memories of a bygone era.

According to the book, The Half Doll, by Shona and Marc Lorrin, porcelain half dolls originated in Germany around the beginning of the 20th century and were known as "useful decoration dolls." By 1910, in Germany, the little ladies had found their way onto many household items such as candy boxes, tea cozies, egg cozies, and electric lamps. Later, during the 1920s and 1930s, the half dolls experienced extreme popularity and were available in many parts of the world. They were often found on items in a lady's home - on powder puff boxes, on lamps, as telephone covers, on brushes, and of course, as pincushions.

This modern reproduction half doll is a pincushion with a dress made from wide ribbons and lace. She holds a ribbon chatelaine pincushion basket and a ribbon needle book. The ribbonwork on the dress is small and "fiddly" but still very easy for the beginner to accomplish. As you work on this project I am sure you will think of other things to add to the half doll's dress. Why not bead the lace overskirt or make a hat for her to carry over her arm instead of the chatelaine pieces? Let the imagination go - be creative and have fun with this. I guarantee that you will want to make more half doll projects after you are finished with this one!

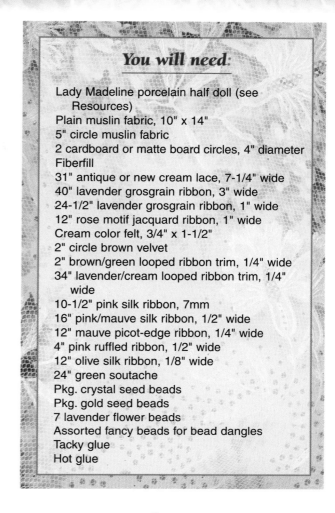

You will need:

Lady Madeline porcelain half doll (see Resources)
Plain muslin fabric, 10" x 14"
5" circle muslin fabric
2 cardboard or matte board circles, 4" diameter
Fiberfill
31" antique or new cream lace, 7-1/4" wide
40" lavender grosgrain ribbon, 3" wide
24-1/2" lavender grosgrain ribbon, 1" wide
12" rose motif jacquard ribbon, 1" wide
Cream color felt, 3/4" x 1-1/2"
2" circle brown velvet
2" brown/green looped ribbon trim, 1/4" wide
34" lavender/cream looped ribbon trim, 1/4" wide
10-1/2" pink silk ribbon, 7mm
16" pink/mauve silk ribbon, 1/2" wide
12" mauve picot-edge ribbon, 1/4" wide
4" pink ruffled ribbon, 1/2" wide
12" olive silk ribbon, 1/8" wide
24" green soutache
Pkg. crystal seed beads
Pkg. gold seed beads
7 lavender flower beads
Assorted fancy beads for bead dangles
Tacky glue
Hot glue

Steps:

Make the bows, flowers, and leaves:
1. Knot flowers: Refer to diagram 4 (page 97) to make eight knot flowers. Use 2" of the 1/2" wide pink/mauve silk ribbon for each. Trim the tails to 1/2" and insert the tails into the holes in the posy on the half doll. A tiny dab of glue under the knot will stop them from popping out.
2. Bows: Refer to diagrams 13a-13b (page 100) to make three, three-loop bows. Use 3-1/2" of 7mm pink silk ribbon for each bow. Finish each bow with a gold seed bead in the center.
3. Coiled rose: Refer to diagrams 18a-18c (page 103) to make one coiled rose. Use 4" of pink ruffled ribbon.
4. Mini roses: Refer to diagram 33 (page 112) to make three mini folded roses, each using 4" of narrow mauve picot-edge ribbon. Coil and gather the last 2" of the ribbon rose around the folded center.
5. Loop leaves: Refer to diagram 11 (page 100) to make eight single loop leaves. Use 1-1/2" of 1/8" wide olive ribbon for each leaf.

Make the pincushion and attach the half doll:

1. Make a tube from the muslin rectangle by sewing the 10" sides together. Close the base of the tube by stitching around the opening and gathering tightly.

2. Glue and insert a 4" cardboard circle inside the closed bottom of the tube.

3. Cover a second cardboard circle with the 5" circle of muslin by stitching around the edge of the fabric and gathering tightly over the cardboard. Refer to Step 3, page 55 in the Hat Pincushion project.

4. Glue this covered circle to the underside of the tube. This helps stabilize the base of the pincushion.

5. Firmly pack the pincushion tube with fiberfill stuffing then stitch around the top and gather tightly to close the tube.

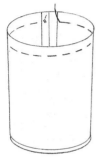

6. Note: The knot flowers must be in the half doll's posy before you can continue (see Step 1, page 29). Slip the half doll over the top of the pincushion and stitch her to it. Use double thread and a straight or curved needle to sew through the sew holes. The pincushion height should measure about 6-1/4" to 6-1/2" tall after it is sewn to the half doll.

Make the ribbon dress and lace overskirt:

1. Dress: The dress is made up of two 20" lengths of 3" wide lavender grosgrain ribbon and one 20" length of 1" wide lavender grosgrain ribbon. Overlap the three pieces of ribbon by 1/8" and stitch them together with very tiny stitches. The finished width will be approximately 6-3/4" wide.

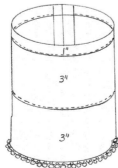

2. Sew the lavender/cream loop trim to the bottom of the dress ribbons. Align the short sides of the joined ribbons, and sew a seam so a tube will be made. Set aside the ribbon dress until the lace overskirt is made.

3. Lace overskirt: Turn under the raw edges of the 7-1/4" sides of lace by 1/8" and gather each side tightly.

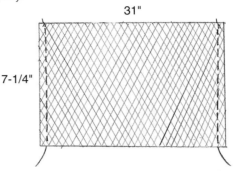

4. Turn under the top edge of the lace if it has a raw edge. Gather the long top edge to fit around the ribbon dress.

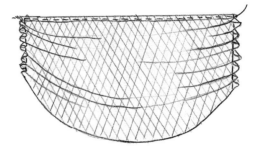

5. Pin the lace overskirt to the ribbon dress. Using double thread, gather around the top edge of both the ribbon dress and the lace overskirt.

6. Place the gathered dress over the half doll, tighten the gathering and secure with stitches. Take a few hidden stitches in the folds of the dress and tack it to the pincushion, near the half doll's waist. If the dress is a bit short, add a row of narrow lace to the bottom.

Decorate the dress:

1. Using the photo as a guide, stitch the roses to the dress; stitch the loop leaves behind the main rose and behind the mini rose.

2. Tack a 21" length of olive green soutache to the dress with small stitches and highlight it with crystal seed beads. Accent the roses and soutache with the seven lavender flower beads.

3. Sew two pink bows to the lace and one pink bow to the chatelaine loop after the chatelaine pieces have been attached.

Make the chatelaine - pincushion basket and needle book:

1. Prepare the loop that the chatelaine attaches to by threading a 3" piece of soutache through the hole in the half doll's arm. Stitch it together and set aside. When the chatelaine pieces have been sewn to the loop, cover the stitched area of the loop with a pink bow.

2. Pincushion basket: Stitch a 3" piece of lavender/cream loop trim to one edge of a 3" piece of jacquard ribbon. Sew the short ends of the ribbons together to make a tube. Stitch around the base of the tube and gather tightly. Turn the tube right side out and bead the base of the basket and the side handles with an assortment of seed beads and faceted beads.

3. Stitch around the edge of the 2" velvet circle. Partially gather so a bowl shape is formed.

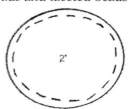

4. Stuff with fiberfill and gather tightly. Sew 2" of green/brown loop trim to the top.

5. Glue this velvet "ball" inside the ribbon basket. Stitch the basket to the green soutache at the half doll's arm.

6. Needle book: Cut two 2-1/4" lengths of 1" wide jacquard ribbon for the covers. Cut two 2-1/4" lengths of 1" wide lavender grosgrain ribbon for the liners. Fold under the raw edges of the ribbons so the finished sides measure 1-3/4" each. Stitch 4-1/2" of lavender/cream loop trim to three sides of each of the jacquard ribbon covers.

7. Stitch a small piece of felt to the front side of one of the lavender ribbon liners.

8. Join the lavender ribbon liners to the jacquard ribbon covers with stitching or fusible webbing.

9. Align the covers and whip stitch them together so the "spine" of the book is formed. Secure the thread in the base of the spine and thread some beads onto the thread. Come back through the beads and secure the thread to the base of the needle book.

10. With a double thread secured in the top of the needle book, thread ten seed beads and stitch to the chatelaine loop. Cover the soutache loop with a pink bow and your half doll pincushion is complete!

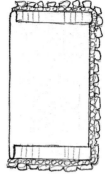

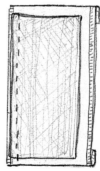

Clara Tassel

Traditionally, a 1920s hanging half doll would have graced the top of a whisk brush or a powder puff patter, so using them as tassels is a new "innovation." The basic model shown here is very simple to make and is a great starting point for adding even more embellishments such as laces and buttons. Go wild and create something extravagant.

And what do you do with the half doll tassel? Hang her from a doorknob or a china cupboard; use her as a curtain tieback or a ceiling fan pull; or keep her as a special ornament for the Christmas tree!

Combine a half doll, some lampshade fringing, ribbon flowers, and beads and you have a stunning tassel.

You will need:

Clara porcelain half doll with tassel hole (see Resources)
10" lampshade fringing, off white or dyed, 6" wide
8" pale green cord or narrow silk ribbon
15" olive green braid or silk satin ribbon, 1/4" wide
12" fuzzy embellishment thread
9" pale green silk satin ribbon, 1/4" wide
27" pale pink bias-cut silk ribbon, 1" wide
6" pink/green ruffled-edge ribbon, 1/4" wide
2" square of crinoline
3 gold seed beads
Optional beadwork:
60 pearl seed beads
30 pearl small bugle beads
3 fancy small round beads
Tacky glue

Steps:

Prepare the half doll:

1. In the cord or narrow silk ribbon, make a loop with a double knot at the end. Insert this knotted loop into the half doll's body so the loop exits at the hole on the top of her head. A dot of glue on the knot will stop the knot from coming out through the head hole. The exposed loop will be the hanger for the finished half doll tassel.

Make the tassel:

1. The fringing I used in this tassel was originally off-white but I dyed it in tea before I rolled it up and put it into the half doll. Make a pot of tea, have a

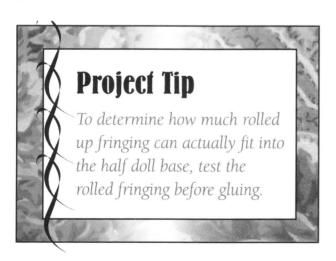

Project Tip

To determine how much rolled up fringing can actually fit into the half doll base, test the rolled fringing before gluing.

cup, then dunk the fringing in the teapot for a few minutes! You might also try using some of the herbal teas which yield other colors - soft pink, creamy yellow, peach, etc. Of course, any fabric dyes will work too. Let the fringing dry overnight or use a hair dryer to speed up the process.

2. Glue the top edge of the fringing with tacky glue and roll it up tightly. Let dry.

Glue →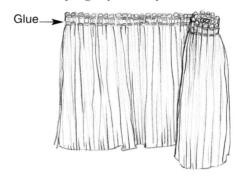

3. Place some glue inside the half doll's waist and insert the fringing. Let dry.

4. Glue a small amount of the fuzzy embellishing thread and cover the base edge of the half doll.

5. Glue the olive green braid or silk ribbon over this thread and so the sew holes are covered. If using the silk ribbon, gather it slightly before applying it to the half doll.

Make the flowers and leaves:

1. Roses: Refer to diagrams 32a-32f (page 111) to make three folded roses, using 9" of pale pink bias-cut silk ribbon for each rose.

2. Pink rosettes: Refer to diagrams 17a and 17d (page 103) to make three small rosettes, using 2" of pink/green ruffled-edge ribbon for each rosette. Cover the centers with one gold seed bead.

3. Leaves: Refer to diagrams 36a-36d (page 114) to make five curved leaves, using 2-1/4" of olive green braid or silk ribbon for each leaf.

Put the composition together on crinoline:

1. Refer to diagram 12 (page 100) to make a small two-loop bow from the pale green silk ribbon. Stitch this to the crinoline.

2. Add a single 8" loop of the fuzzy embellishing thread on top of the bow.

3. In an arrangement that is pleasing to you, stitch the three roses, five leaves, and three rosettes to the crinoline. As an optional feature to this tassel, incorporate two or three bead dangles.

Lady Eleanor
Lavender Sachet

*B*y adapting the half doll tassel you can create this sweet and fragrant half doll sachet. Under her rose-embellished ribbon and lace skirt she hides a lavender bag. Take a closer look at the green loop trim with yellow roses - this is something you will make! Start with a plain base of purchased green loop ribbon trim and embellish it with handmade ribbon roses and beads. This is fiddly but well worth the effort!

Use this half doll sachet to freshen a room by hanging her on a doorknob or from a decorative hanger on the wall.

Ribbons, trims, antique lace, and a sachet of lavender buds makes up this stunning half doll.

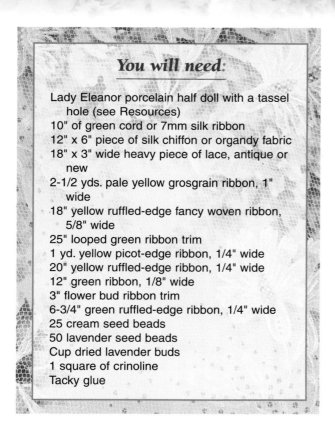

You will need:

Lady Eleanor porcelain half doll with a tassel hole (see Resources)
10" of green cord or 7mm silk ribbon
12" x 6" piece of silk chiffon or organdy fabric
18" x 3" wide heavy piece of lace, antique or new
2-1/2 yds. pale yellow grosgrain ribbon, 1" wide
18" yellow ruffled-edge fancy woven ribbon, 5/8" wide
25" looped green ribbon trim
1 yd. yellow picot-edge ribbon, 1/4" wide
20" yellow ruffled-edge ribbon, 1/4" wide
12" green ribbon, 1/8" wide
3" flower bud ribbon trim
6-3/4" green ruffled-edge ribbon, 1/4" wide
25 cream seed beads
50 lavender seed beads
Cup dried lavender buds
1 square of crinoline
Tacky glue

Steps:

Prepare the half doll:

1. Use the cord or narrow silk ribbon to make a loop with a double knot at the end. Insert this knotted loop into the half doll's body so the loop exits at the hole on the top of her head. A dot of glue on the knot will stop the knot from coming out through the head hole. The exposed loop becomes the hanger for the finished half doll sachet.

Make the sachet:

1. Fold the 12" x 6" piece of fabric in half and sew up the side seams. Turn inside out and fill the bag with lavender buds.

2. Close the bag by stitching around the top, 1" down from the edge. If the top of the lavender bag is too loose a fit for the half doll cavity, simply glue some leftover fabric around the top of the bag until it fits snugly inside the doll.

3. Apply some glue to the top of the bag and inside the half doll's waist. Insert the bag into the half doll. For extra stability, stitch the bag to the half doll through the sew holes. Set aside.

Make the roses and leaves:

1. Small roses: Refer to diagrams 32a-32f (page 111) to make seven tiny folded roses, using 2-1/4" of yellow picot-edge ribbon for each rose. Trim the excess ribbon closely. Refer to the photo for placement and stitch six roses to the green loop ribbon trim. The remaining rose is used in the waist corsage.

2. Large roses: Refer to Rose #1 in the Combination Rose Guide (page 118). Make eight roses. The folded rose center uses 2-1/4" of yellow picot ribbon. The single u-gather outer petals use 2-1/2" of yellow ruffled-edge ribbon. Refer to the photo for placement and stitch seven roses to the green loop ribbon trim. The remaining rose is used in the waist corsage.

3. Leaves: Refer to diagrams 36a-36d (page 114) to make three curved leaves, using 2-1/4" of olive green ruffled-edge ribbon for each leaf.

Make the ribbon and lace skirt:

1. Cut two 36" pieces of 1" wide yellow grosgrain. Refer to diagram 5 (page 97) and gather each piece along the edges to a length of 18".

2. With small running stitches, join one of these shirred pieces to the top edge of the 3" wide lace and the other to the bottom edge of the lace.

Small combination roses and beaded trim embellish a spectacular half doll's dress.

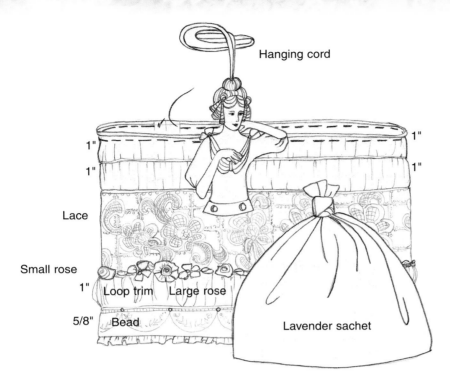

Hanging cord

1"

1"

1"

1"

Lace

Small rose

1" Loop trim Large rose

5/8" Bead

Lavender sachet

3. Stitch an 18" flat piece of yellow grosgrain ribbon to the top shirred ribbon.

4. Stitch the 18" piece of yellow ruffled-edge fancy woven ribbon to the bottom shirred ribbon.

5. Bead the top edge of the fancy yellow woven ribbon with cream seed beads, approximately 1" apart.

6. Bead the green loop trim (six small and seven large yellow roses should now be stitched to it) with three lavender seed beads at the center of every loop motif.

7. Stitch the green loop trim to the dress as shown in the photo. The dress "fabric" is now ready to be constructed into a dress.

8. Refer to diagrams 16a-16b (page 101) and fold the "fabric" in half to make a tube. Turn right side out.

9. Using double thread, gather the top edge of the dress, slip it over the half doll, and secure the gathering tightly.

10. Secure the dress to the lavender bag with a few hidden stitches in the folds of the dress near the half doll's waist.

11. Bead 4" of green loop trim with lavender seed beads, as before, and stitch this embellished trim to the dress waist.

Make the waist corsage:

1. Make a simple shoelace bow from the 1/8" wide green ribbon. Tie knots in the streamers.

2. Stitch this bow to a 1" square of crinoline.

3. Referring to the photo, stitch one large rose and one small rose to the crinoline. Surround the large rose with the 3" piece of lavender flower bud ribbon trim. Add three leaves.

4. Trim the excess crinoline and stitch the corsage to the dress near the half doll's waist.

Project Tip

If you want a very finished dress, line the back of the pieced "ribbon fabric" with a piece of silk chiffon.

Chapter 3

Brooches With Flair

Brown Brooch   Page 38

Peach Brooch   Page 41

Autumn Brooch   Page 44

Brown Brooch

Wide jacquard ribbon is used as the background on this brooch. A silk rose, pansy, raspberry blossoms, rosettes, and berries blend together to create a magical ribbon garden.

Over time, you will accumulate many odds and ends of ribbons, beads, and trims. Hang on to them all because one day you will need them! Such was the case with this brooch. When you look at the supply list for this brooch you will see that it is mostly bits and pieces of trims and ribbons. The brooch also reflects a wide variety of ribbons - jacquard ribbon, ruffled trims, velvet ribbon, wire-edge ribbon, silk ribbon, in addition to many beads and buttons. Go through your own stash of bits and pieces and see what you can come up with to make a brooch using this project as a guideline.

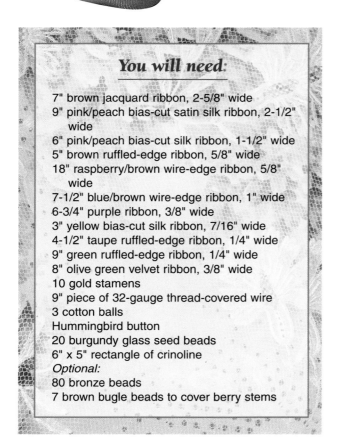

You will need:

7" brown jacquard ribbon, 2-5/8" wide
9" pink/peach bias-cut satin silk ribbon, 2-1/2" wide
6" pink/peach bias-cut silk ribbon, 1-1/2" wide
5" brown ruffled-edge ribbon, 5/8" wide
18" raspberry/brown wire-edge ribbon, 5/8" wide
7-1/2" blue/brown wire-edge ribbon, 1" wide
6-3/4" purple ribbon, 3/8" wide
3" yellow bias-cut silk ribbon, 7/16" wide
4-1/2" taupe ruffled-edge ribbon, 1/4" wide
9" green ruffled-edge ribbon, 1/4" wide
8" olive green velvet ribbon, 3/8" wide
10 gold stamens
9" piece of 32-gauge thread-covered wire
3 cotton balls
Hummingbird button
20 burgundy glass seed beads
6" x 5" rectangle of crinoline
Optional:
80 bronze beads
7 brown bugle beads to cover berry stems

Steps:

Prepare the background:

1. Prepare the brooch background using three layers of crinoline, 3" x 2-1/2" each, and the brown jacquard ribbon. With large basting stitches in a contrasting thread color, attach the crinoline to the wrong side of the jacquard ribbon. The "image area" you have to work with on the front of the brown ribbon is the area inside the basting stitches. Set aside.

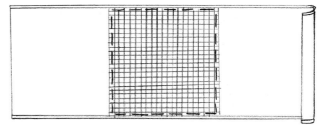

Make the flowers and leaves:

1. Rose: Refer to Rose #13b in the Combination Rose Guide (page 121), to make one rose, using 6" of 1-1/2" wide pink/peach silk ribbon folded in half for the rose center. Use 3" of 2-1/2" wide pink/peach silk ribbon folded in half for each of the three rose petals. The folded rose is stitched to a 5/8" circle of crinoline. Stitch the single u-gather petals in place, over the folded rose center and under the crinoline.

2. Purple pansy: Refer to diagrams 23a-23b (page 105) to make the two-petal back for one miniature pansy, using 2-3/4" of the narrow purple ribbon. Refer to diagrams 24a-24c (page 106) to make the three-petal front, using 4" of purple ribbon. Before stitching the front petal piece to the back petal piece, make a knot with 3" of yellow silk ribbon and insert it into the front petals.

3. Berries: Refer to diagrams 16a-16e (page 101) to make three berries, using 2-1/2" of blue/brown ribbon and 3" of 32-gauge wire for each berry. Optional: Embellish the wire stem of each berry with three brown bugle beads. Join the berries by twisting their wires together.

4. Raspberry blossoms: Refer to diagrams 7a-7e (page 98) to make two ruched blossoms, using 9" of raspberry/brown wire-edge ribbon for each. The spacing for the ruching is 1-1/2". Refer to diagram 1 (page 96) and insert five stamens in each blossom.

5. Taupe rosettes: Refer to diagrams 17a and 17d (page 103) to make two rosettes, using 2-1/4" of taupe ruffled ribbon for each rosette. Cover the center with three burgundy seed beads.

6. Half-boat leaves: Refer to diagrams 38a-38e (page 116) to make four half-boat leaves, using 2-1/4" of ruffled-edge green ribbon for each leaf.

7. Curved leaves: Refer to diagrams 36a-36d (page 114) to make two curved leaves, using 4" of the velvet ribbon for each leaf.

8. Brown ruffle: With very tiny stitches, slightly gather the brown ruffled-edge ribbon just enough so that it curves easily. The ruffle is the first element to be sewn to the jacquard ribbon. Turn back the raw edges and tack the ruffle to the jacquard ribbon. Secure the ruffle with several burgundy seed beads at intervals along its curve.

Put the composition together:

1. Using the photo as a guide, stitch all the elements to the front of the jacquard ribbon, within the "image area" in the following order: brown ruffle arch, rose, two large leaves, three berries, two blossoms, four small leaves, two rosettes, one pansy, and the hummingbird button.

Finish the brooch:

1. The finished brooch size is about 3-1/8" wide x 2-5/8" deep. Turn back the jacquard ribbon so it covers the back of the brooch. Turn under one raw edge and slipstitch the overlapped edge. Whip stitch the top and bottom edges of the brooch to close the brown ribbon.

2. Sew a large pin back to the back.

3. Bead the bottom of the brooch in a manner pleasing to you. The beading pattern shown in the photo uses three loops of assorted beads. Use a double thread and attach it to the end of the brooch, string on the number of beads needed to form a loop and sew the string to the brooch. Repeat for as many loops of beads as you need.

Peach Brooch

This sweet little arrangement of new ribbon flowers is exquisite on a vintage satin handkerchief case.

A vintage French button, with the tiniest spray of lily of the valley on it, was the inspiration for this ribbon flower composition. Being only 3-1/2" in diameter, this composition is perfect for many uses. Originally intended to be a brooch, I found that the design looked very nice as an embellishment on a pillow as well as on this vintage handkerchief case. Because of the size ribbons used, this project will be tricky and somewhat fiddly to make, but the results are well worth it. If you love miniature work you will love this and if not... well, then perhaps come back to this after you are comfortable working with the larger ribbon projects.

You will need:

10" thread-covered wire, 22-gauge
9" thread-covered wire, 32-gauge
18" olive green bias-cut silk ribbon, 5/8" wide
28" peach satin-edged georgette ribbon, 5/8" wide
10" olive green velvet ribbon, 1/8" wide
18" peach/cream ombre wire-edge ribbon, 1" wide
18" dark peach ribbon, 3/4" wide
6" cream wire-edge ribbon, 5/8" wide
12" lavender wire-edge ribbon, 5/8" wide
12" off-white satin-edged georgette ribbon, 1/8" wide
9" brown/green ombre wire-edge ribbon, 1" wide
9" olive green ombre wire-edge ribbon, 1" wide
10" mint green picot-edge ribbon, 1/2" wide
7" pale green ruffled-edge ribbon, 1/2" wide
9" olive green picot-edge ribbon, 1/4" wide
8" lime green picot-edge ribbon, 1/4" wide
6" square of crinoline
4 green glass leaf beads
7 small faceted peach glass beads
5 tiny round ecru glass beads
Vintage button, 1-1/16" diameter (or element of your choice)
Tacky glue

Steps:

Make the round framework:

1. Bend the 10" piece of 22-gauge wire into a circle, overlapping the ends 1", and glue the ends together. Wrap the join with 2" of lightly glued green bias-cut silk ribbon. Let dry.

2. Apply a thin coat of tacky glue around the wire circle and wrap the wire with 15" of the green bias-cut silk ribbon. Set aside.

3. Refer to diagram 9 (page 99) and pleat 20" of the peach georgette ribbon, making each pleat about 3/8" wide. This will yield about 8" to 9" of pleated ribbon.

4. Stitch the pleated ribbon to the covered wire circle. It will only cover about 2/3 of the wire circle.

5. Stitch the wire circle to the 6" piece of crinoline.

6. Using the 10" piece of olive green velvet ribbon, create a "vine" by twisting and looping the ribbon in a random manner in the same area as the pleated peach ribbon, but on top of the wire circle. Secure the vine with stitches and set aside.

Make the flowers:

1. **Lilies of the valley**: Refer to diagram 16i (page 102) to make three lilies of the valley, using 2" of cream wire-edge ribbon and 3" of 32-gauge wire for each.

2. **Peach roses**: Refer to Rose #2a in the Combination Rose Guide (page 118) to make two cabochon roses. The folded rose center uses 6" of the dark peach ribbon. The three outer petals use 2" each of the peach/cream wire-edge ribbon. The folded rose is stitched to a 1/2" circle of crinoline. Stitch the single u-gather petals in place, over the folded rose center and under the crinoline.

3. **Peach rosebuds**: Refer to diagrams 18a-18c (page 103) to make three coiled rosebuds, using 2" of the dark peach ribbon for each. These are tiny! Note: The ribbon is folded in half so its width is only 3/8" wide and the gathering is very slight.

4. **Pale peach rose**: Refer to Rose #17 in the Combination Rose Guide (page 121) to make one pale peach rose. The rose center uses 6" of peach/cream wire-edge ribbon. The outer petals use 8" of the peach georgette ribbon. Make the outer petals first and then the center. Stitch the twisted, coiled center on top of the five petals.

5. **Purple sweet peas**: Refer to diagrams 20a-20c (page 104) to make five sweet peas, using 2-1/4" of lavender ribbon for each flower. Style the sweet peas

by fanning out the back ruffle and pinching the front ruffle at its top.

6. Cream rosettes: Refer to diagrams 17a and 17d (page 103) to make five cream rosettes, using 2-1/4" of narrow off-white georgette ribbon for each rosette. Sew one small ecru bead to the center of each rosette.

7. Prairie point leaves: Refer to diagrams 35a-35d (page 113) to make six prairie point leaves, using 3" of olive green ombre ribbon for three of the leaves and 3" of brown/green ombre ribbon for the other three leaves.

8. Boat leaves: Refer to diagrams 37a-37d (page 115) to make two boat leaves, using 5" of sheer mint green picot-edge ribbon for each.

9. Half-boat leaves: Refer to diagrams 38a-38e (page 116) to make three half-boat leaves, using 2-1/4" of pale green ruffled-edge ribbon for each. Make another three half-boat leaves, using 3" of the 1/4" olive green picot-edge ribbon for each. Make four more half-boat leaves, using 2" of lime green picot-edge ribbon for each.

Put the composition together:

1. This is an off-center arrangement. Remember to work from the back of the composition forward. Refer to the photo for most of the placement of the flowers and leaves. Begin with the two large sheer leaves, followed with the button (or element of your choice) on top.

2. The three roses overlap the button and have four of the prairie point leaves under them. Tuck in a few of the smaller leaves and rosettes on top of the larger leaves.

3. Working away from the focal point, add the three lilies of the valley, leaves, sweet peas, rosebuds, and rosettes.

4. Sew on the glass leaf beads near the smallest ribbon leaves.

5. Embellish the vine with the peach glass beads.

Finish the composition:

Very carefully trim the excess crinoline away from all the outer and inner edges of the composition. If you intend to use this as a brooch, you will need to finish the back by covering the crinoline with some Ultrasuede or wool felt and sew a pin back to it. If you are using the composition on a pillow or having it framed, you needn't do anything to the back.

Miniature lilies of the valley, leaves, sweet peas, cabochon roses, and rosettes surround a vintage French button.

Autumn Brooch

This classic brooch is a rich composition of roses, rosehips, feathers, beads, and leaves.

It is very rewarding to incorporate many elements into your ribbonwork. This project is rich with different ribbons, colors, textures, and shapes. With the addition of the chenille trim, the feathers and the yellow chandelier "dingle," it makes for a very beautiful composition. Be imaginative - there are no rules!

You will need:

13" gold ombre wire-edge ribbon, 1-1/2" wide
6" gold ribbon, 5/8" wide
13" raspberry/cinnamon ombre wire-edge ribbon, 1" wide
9" green velvet ribbon, 1" wide
10" flower bud chenille trim, 1/4" wide
10-1/2" olive green ombre wire-edge ribbon, 1-1/2" wide
6" gold/green wire-edge ribbon, 1" wide
7" purple wire-edge ribbon, 5/8" wide
16 yellow/red stamens
6" olive green bias-cut silk ribbon, 5/8" wide
18" thread-covered wire, 32-gauge
5 velvet millinery leaves
3 small pheasant feathers
Lace leaf motif
Gold leaf charm
4" square of crinoline
Tacky glue
Optional:
Vintage "fuzzy" stamen
Assortment of glass beads - seeds, leaves, bugles, faceted rounds, dagger beads

Steps:

Make the flowers and leaves:

1. Gold rose: Refer to Rose #6 in the Combination Rose Guide (page 119). Use 6" of unwired gold ribbon for the center. Use 13" of gold ombre wire-edge ribbon for the outer petals. Fold the ribbon so its width is 1" wide. The spacing for the five-petal u-gather is 1/4" seam allowance and petal spacing of 2-1/2" each.

2. Purple blossom: Refer to diagrams 25a-25b (page 106) to make one blossom, using 7" of purple wire-edge ribbon. Insert four double-headed yellow/red stamens in the center of the petals.

3. Rosehips: Refer to diagrams 16a-16e (page 101) to make five stemmed rosehips, using 2-1/2" of raspberry/cinnamon wire-edge ribbon and 3" of wire for each.

4. Spent rose stamens: Refer to diagram 2 (page 96) and join eight double-headed yellow/red stamens together with 3" of 32-gauge wire. Cover the wire with the 6" length of olive green bias-cut silk ribbon.

5. Prairie point leaves: Refer to diagrams 35a-35d (page 113) to make three prairie point leaves, using 3-1/2" of olive green ombre wire-edge ribbon for each leaf.

6. Mitered leaves: Refer to diagrams 39a-39d (page 117) to make two mitered leaves, using 3" of gold/green wire-edge ribbon for each leaf.

7. Velvet loops with chenille trim: Cut the green velvet ribbon into two 4-1/2" pieces. Fold it in half so a loop is formed. Align the raw edges of the ribbon together and secure the loops together. Cut the chenille trim into two 5" pieces. Place one piece of chenille trim over each velvet loop and stitch in place at the top of the loop and at the bottom of the loop. Trim off the excess chenille.

Put the composition together on crinoline:

1. Referring to the photo for placement, begin by stitching the five millinery leaves to the 4" square of crinoline.

2. Stitch on the velvet loops, followed by the gold rose. Tuck in the large leaves and the smaller leaves.

3. Stitch together the pheasant feathers and tack them near the top of the arrangement. Add the blossom, the spent rose stamens, and the rosehips.

4. Embellish with the lace leaf motif and the gold leaf charm.

Finish the composition:

1. After all the elements of the composition have been stitched in place, clip away the excess crinoline.

2. Cover the back of the brooch with a piece of Ultrasuede, thin leather, or wool felt.

3. Stitch a pin back to the back. The brooch can be used on a pillow, as a framed piece, or pinned to a coat or hat. Your choice!

Chapter 4
Hats and More

"For street wear the cloche shape lingers but the long efforts of the designers to change its vogue are apparently bearing fruit. A number of ateliers are already showing advanced models which approach the picture hats of past seasons in size and lavish trimmings." The Milliner, April 1924. This old-fashioned description of hats was the inspiration behind several of the new wide-brimmed hats shown in this photo. But don't be fooled into thinking these are all new hats. Look closely and see if you can spot the 1920s hat!

Pink Hat With Rose

A cocarde made of French ribbon, a ribbon tea rose, a glass button, and some lace comprise this magnificent hat.

French milliner's catalogue and invitation to view the 1909 autumn collection.

*O*ver the last few years I have enjoyed researching the topic of millinery and am thrilled (or as my friend Phyllis says, "all a twitterpatter!") when I come across some wonderful item of millinery memorabilia. The French postcard and the French milliner's catalogue were particularly great finds as they related to two eras in which I am most interested - late Victorian and Edwardian.

Inspired by many of the antique hats that I've seen, the hat in this project is a combination of some of those styles. It doesn't really fit into any one time period. It was just fun to create. Trimming this hat is very simple to do. You'll need a medium-brimmed fabric hat (a straw hat might work too), some lace, wide ribbon, and a spray of vintage milliner's leaves. I added a hand-painted glass button for extra interest.

Enjoy wearing your hat - yes wear it! Don't have a tea party to go to? Then start a tea club in your area and invite some friends to tea.

You will need:

Fabric hat
1 yd. lace with decorative edge, 7" wide
36" pink grosgrain ribbon, 3" wide
12" pink grosgrain ribbon, 1-1/2" wide
12" pale pink bias-cut silk ribbon, 1-1/2" wide
56" pale pink bias-cut silk ribbon, 2-1/2" wide
Glass button, 1-3/4" diameter
Vintage spray of milliner's leaves
3" square of crinoline

Steps:

Make the two cocardes:

1. **Large cocarde**: Refer to diagram 10 (page 99). Leaving about 4" at each end of the 36" piece of wide pink grosgrain ribbon, divide and pin the ribbon into 14 pleats. Each pleat is 1" and overlaps by 1/2". Fan out the pleats before stitching them in place with two rows of stitching. Fold the raw edges of the tails under and slipstitch in place.

At the milliners, French postcard circa 1900.

2. Small cocarde: Refer to diagram 10 (page 99) to make ten pleats in the 1-1/2" wide pink grosgrain ribbon, each one is 1/2" and overlapping by 1/4". Fold the raw edges under and slipstitch in place. Fan out the pleats and stitch with one row of stitches.

3. Stitch the large cocarde in a horseshoe shape to the 3" crinoline square. Stitch the small cocarde opposite this. Sew a glass button over the small cocarde.

4. Trim the excess crinoline from the back of the cocarde composition. Set aside until the tea rose is made.

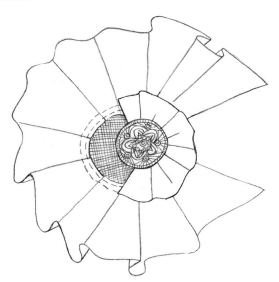

Make the ribbon tea rose:

1. Refer to Rose #12 in the Combination Rose Guide (page 120). Use 12" of 1-1/2" wide silk ribbon for the coiled rose center and 12" of 2-1/2" wide silk ribbon for three rolled corner petals (each petal uses 4"). Use 44" of 2-1/2" wide silk ribbon for eight rolled corner petals (each petal uses 5-1/2"). Stitch all the smaller petals to the coiled rose center first. Overlap and stitch the eight larger petals around the smaller petals in a clockwise direction. Complete the rose by trimming the excess ribbon from the base of the rose.

2. Stitch the rose to the empty space on the cocarde composition.

Trim the hat:

1. The hat decorations can be placed at the front of the hat or in the back. You decide which you like best. Drape one yard of lace around the hat brim in a pleasing manner. The seam will be covered by the cocarde and tea rose composition. Secure the lace in a few places with stitches.

2. Pin the cocarde and rose composition on the hat.

3. Pin the millinery leaves under this. Arrange as desired, then stitch in place.

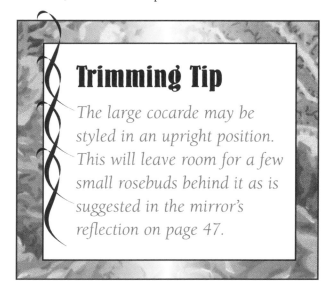

Trimming Tip

The large cocarde may be styled in an upright position. This will leave room for a few small rosebuds behind it as is suggested in the mirror's reflection on page 47.

Purple Hat

A looped milliner's bow topped off with bright little ribbon flowers makes this a stunning 1920s style hat.

According to The Milliner *magazine, April 1924, "The topic of ribbon trimmings is inexhaustible, and there are very few hats, indeed, that do not feature at least a touch of ribbon in one form or another, no matter how trimmed otherwise. The cockade is still in high favour and... for more dressy chapeaux there are intricate arrangements of loops and torsades, all very charming and interesting."*

The little number displayed here is a version of a cloche with a small brim, stylishly trimmed with an arresting milliner's bow and charming ribbon flowers. Very much en vogue! Who could resist!

You will need:

Fabric hat
68" purple wire-edge edge ribbon, 2-1/2" wide
12" ivory bias-cut silk ribbon, 1" wide
12" pink bias-cut silk ribbon, 1" wide
12" dark pink bias-cut silk ribbon, 1" wide
12" purple bias-cut silk ribbon, 5/8" wide
6" yellow bias-cut silk ribbon, 5/8" wide
10-1/2" pale blue silk ribbon, 7mm
7-1/2" sheer green wire-edge ribbon, 1" wide
7-1/2" olive green wire-edge ribbon, 1" wide
5" hunter green wire-edge ribbon, 1" wide
6-3/4" pale green satin silk ribbon, 3/8" wide
6-3/4" mint green ruffled-edge ribbon, 1/4" wide
3" sage green soutache
6 yellow seed beads
5" square of crinoline

Steps:

1. Measure around the crown of the hat, cut about 23" of purple ribbon for a hatband, and stitch the ribbon to the crown. Position the seam at the side, under the milliner's bow.

This composition of roses, petunias, dandelion, and forget-me-nots is designed in a gentle curve.

Make the milliner's bow:
1. Refer to diagram 14 (page 100) and use 45" of the purple ribbon. Wrap thread around the ribbon at 9" intervals. Fan out the loops and stitch the bow to the hatband.

Make the flowers and leaves:
1. Roses: Refer to diagrams 32a-32f (page 111) to make three folded roses, using 12" of ivory, dark pink, and pink silk ribbon for each rose.
2. Petunias: Refer to diagrams 17a and 17e (page 103) to make two petunias, using 6" of the purple silk ribbon for each flower. Cover the center of the petunias with three yellow beads.
3. Dandelion: Refer to diagrams 19a-19b (page 104) to make one dandelion, using 6" of yellow bias-cut silk ribbon.
4. Forget-me-nots: Refer to diagrams 25a and 25d (page 106) to make three blue forget-me-nots, using 3-1/2" of pale blue 7mm silk ribbon for each flower. Cover the centers with one small yellow seed bead.
5. Prairie point leaves: Refer to diagrams 35a-35d (page 113) to make eight prairie point leaves. Make three sheer green leaves, three olive green leaves, and two hunter green leaves, using 2-1/2" of ribbon for each leaf.
6. Curved leaves: Refer to diagrams 36a-36d (page 114) to make six curved leaves. Make three mint green leaves and three pale green leaves, using 2-1/4" for each leaf.

Put the composition together on crinoline:
1. Using the photo as a guide, stitch all the elements to the crinoline in the following order:
Roses, petunias, large leaves, small leaves, dandelion and forget-me-nots. Note: The three pale green silk leaves have stems made of soutache. Stitch the soutache to the crinoline and stitch the leaves on top.
2. When all the elements have been stitched on the crinoline, cut away the excess crinoline and stitch the composition to the front of the milliner's bow.

Black Hat With Brown Rose and Feathers

The large brown ribbon rose is the focal point of this Victorian inspired hat. The Victorian silk dress, shoes, and beaded purse are family pieces that were kindly loaned by Emily Gibb.

Don't you admire the workmanship that went into clothing from Victorian times? I do. The velvet-trimmed silk skirt and bodice shown with this hat were very inspiring to me. While not in good condition, I still loved the fabric, its colors and pattern, thus resulting in this hat trimmed with a huge brown ribbon rose and blue/brown blossoms. Perhaps you have something in your old cedar chest that will inspire you to design some ribbon flowers for a hat. (Oh, and don't you love the shoes? They are a size 4A!)

Interior view of the Kaufman Millinery showroom, New Orleans, Louisiana. Postcard circa 1900.

You will need:

Black felt hat
91" brown wire-edge taffeta ribbon, 3" wide
8" dark blue pleated ribbon, 1-1/2" wide
32" blue/brown ombre wire-edge ribbon, 1" wide
16 aqua blue double-headed stamens
Pre-made feather spray, 6" tall

Steps:

Make the flowers:

1. **Brown rose**: Refer to Rose #3 in the Combination Rose Guide (page 118). Use 20" of wide brown ribbon for the folded rose center and 9" for each of the five petals. Arrange the five petals around the folded rose - slightly off-center - and stitch in place. Note: Be sure the rose center does not rise up too high above the petals. Trim the excess ribbon down to 1/4" at the base of the rose.

2. **Blue/brown blossom**: Refer to diagrams 25a-25b (page 106) to make four blossoms, using 8" of the blue/brown ombre ribbon and four aqua blue double-headed stamens for each blossom. Refer to diagram 1 (page 96) for the stamens.

Trim the hat:

1. Loosely twist and drape the remaining brown taffeta ribbon around the crown as a hatband. Position the join in the back and secure it to the crown with stitches.

2. Turn up the back brim of the hat and stitch it to the crown.

3. Stitch the fan of feathers to the turned up brim and set aside.

4. With gathering stitches on the bottom edge of the dark blue pleated ribbon, create a half circle. Stitch this half circle over the base of the feathers.

5. Sew the brown rose close to the half circle but so the blue ribbon shows.

6. Stitch three of the blue/brown blossoms on the brim and one on the crown.

Project Tip

To further embellish this hat you could add a spray of black velvet millinery leaves to the crown, and another pleated half circle with button to the hatband.

Miniature hat pincushions pose as real hats.

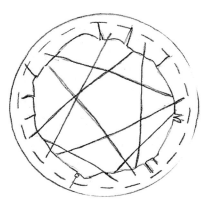

It was fun to design and make these different versions of a hat needle case/pincushion. The basic instructions are the same for all the hats - only the decoration varies. Be creative with your choice of fabrics and don't be afraid to use very expensive ribbons - you will only need inches! The supply list is for the cream hat.

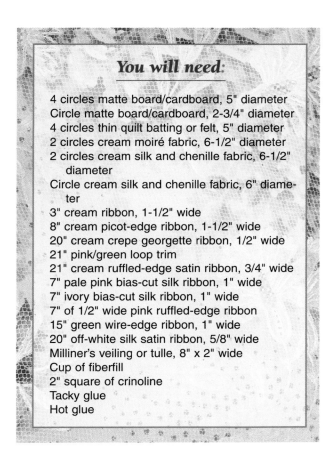

You will need:

4 circles matte board/cardboard, 5" diameter
Circle matte board/cardboard, 2-3/4" diameter
4 circles thin quilt batting or felt, 5" diameter
2 circles cream moiré fabric, 6-1/2" diameter
2 circles cream silk and chenille fabric, 6-1/2" diameter
Circle cream silk and chenille fabric, 6" diameter
3" cream ribbon, 1-1/2" wide
8" cream picot-edge ribbon, 1-1/2" wide
20" cream crepe georgette ribbon, 1/2" wide
21" pink/green loop trim
21" cream ruffled-edge satin ribbon, 3/4" wide
7" pale pink bias-cut silk ribbon, 1" wide
7" ivory bias-cut silk ribbon, 1" wide
7" of 1/2" wide pink ruffled-edge ribbon
15" green wire-edge ribbon, 1" wide
20" off-white silk satin ribbon, 5/8" wide
Milliner's veiling or tulle, 8" x 2" wide
Cup of fiberfill
2" square of crinoline
Tacky glue
Hot glue

Steps:

Make the hat needle case/pincushion:

1. Glue one circle of batting to one 5" cardboard circle. Repeat for the remaining three 5" cardboard circles.

2. Sew gathering stitches 1/4" from the edge of each of the four fabric circles.

3. Place a stitched fabric circle over the batting on each of the cardboard circles. Tighten the gathering and secure as shown.

4. Set the two cream moiré covered circles side by side, face down, and "join" them together by gluing the 3" piece of 1-1/2" wide cream ribbon to the wrong side of the boards - this is the hinge.

5. Turn the joined boards over, right side up, and place 7" of cream ruffled-edge satin ribbon across each of the boards - these are the needle holders. Glue them in place on the back of the boards.

6. Glue a 10" piece of 5/8" wide off-white silk satin ribbon to each side of the joined boards - these are the hat closures.

7. Hot glue the chenille/silk covered circles to the cream moiré circles (wrong sides together). This completes the needle case portion of the hat pincushion.

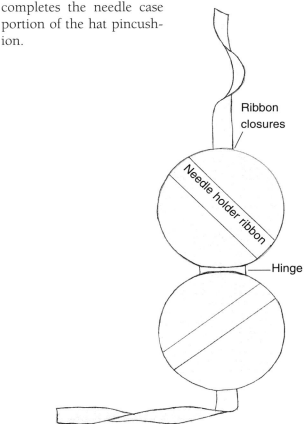

Ribbon closures

Needle holder ribbon

Hinge

8. Sew gathering stitches 1/4" from the edge of the 6" circle of chenille/silk fabric.

9. Loosely draw in the gathering and tightly fill the cavity with fiberfill.

10. Insert the 2-3/4" cardboard circle in top, tighten the gathering, and secure the stitching. This forms the pincushion (crown of hat).

11. Hot glue the crown to the center of the top of the needle case.

Make the bow, flowers, and leaves:

1. Bow: Make a simple two-loop bow - like a bow tie - using 8" of the cream picot-edge ribbon. Tightly gather across the center.

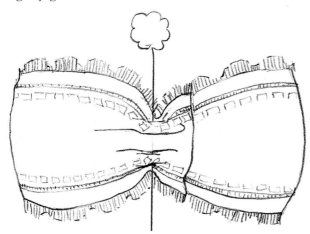

2. Folded roses: Refer to diagrams 32a-32f (page 111) to make three folded roses, using 7" of ribbon for each rose from three different ribbons - cream ruffled-edge satin, ivory silk, and pale pink silk.

3. Pink roses: Refer to diagrams 18a-18c (page 103) to make three coiled roses, using 2-1/4" of pink ruffled-edge ribbon for each rose.

4. Loops: Refer to diagram 11 (page 100) to make three single loops, using 3" of pink/green loop trim for each loop.

5. Leaves: Refer to diagrams 35a-35d (page 113) to make five prairie point leaves, using 3" of green wire-edge ribbon for each.

Make the composition:

1. Gather the veiling along the 8" edge. Referring to the photo, stitch the veiling to the 2" piece of crinoline, then stitch on the bow.

2. Stitch five leaves in a circle and cover them with three folded roses.

3. Tuck in three pink roses and three loops. Trim the excess crinoline.

Trim the hat:

1. Refer to diagram 6 (page 98) and gather 20" of cream crepe georgette ribbon for the hatband.

2. Place this around the crown and secure with stitches.

3. Add 10" of pink/green loop trim on top of this hatband so it falls into the ruffles of the cream ribbon.

4. Stitch the floral composition to the base of the crown at the back of the hat.

Floral Hatpin Holder

Antique German porcelain half dolls admire the variety of ribbon roses and blossoms that decorate the front of a shoe hatpin holder.

The choice of base for this floral arrangement is up to you. Consider an old shoe - the one your great grandmother wore at her wedding would be wonderful, or perhaps use the flowers on a lampshade, on a box top, or attach them to a Victorian-style fabric purse. Whatever you decide to do, the result will be wonderful.

You will need:

Vintage shoe
9" by 12" piece wine velvet fabric
12" sheer wine ribbon, 3" wide
36" sheer wine ribbon, 1-1/2" wide
22" wine ombre wire-edge ribbon, 1" wide
3" wine ruffled-gold-edge ribbon, 1/4" wide
12" wine sheer ribbon, 1" wide
11" mauve ruffled-edge satin ribbon, 3/4" wide
12" pale pink bias-cut silk ribbon, 5/8" wide
9" cream wire-edge ribbon, 1" wide
4" lace, 5/8" wide
4" gold ribbon, 1/2" wide
9" olive ruffled-edge satin ribbon, 1-1/4" wide
15" olive green ombre wire-edge ribbon, 1" wide
6" olive green pleated satin ribbon, 1" wide
Antique gold button, 1/2" diameter
5 double-headed gold stamens
7 pink seed beads
7 pearl seed beads
3" x 4" piece of crinoline
1/2" circle of crinoline
Fiberfill

Steps:

Make the velvet sock:

1. Make a sock pattern by using a tube sock from your dresser drawer.
2. Fold the velvet in half along its length. Lay the sock against the fold of the velvet and cut out the shape and length needed for your shoe. Sew up the seams, leaving one end open.
3. Tightly pack the velvet sock with fiberfill, fold in the end and slipstitch it closed. Insert the sock into the shoe.

Decorate the shoe:

1. Make a simple bow-tie style bow from the 3" wide sheer wine ribbon. Sew this to the crinoline rectangle and set aside.

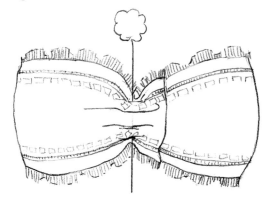

2. Refer to diagram 6 (page 98) and gather the 1-1/2" wide sheer wine ribbon to a length to fit around your shoe. Stitch or glue it to the top edge of the shoe.

Make the flowers and leaves:

1. **Wild rose**: Refer to Rose #16 in the Combination Rose Guide (page 121). This rose has five petals, each made with 2" of 1" wide wine ombre ribbon. The rose center uses 3" of wine gold-edge ribbon. After the rose petals are made, stitch them to a 1/2" circle of crinoline. Cover the center with the antique gold button and add the wine gold-edge ruffle around the button.
2. **Double folded rose**: Refer to diagrams 32a-32f (page 111) to make one folded rose using two ribbons. Use 12" of 1" wide wine sheer ribbon and 12" of wine ombre ribbon together.
3. **Mauve rose**: Refer to diagram 33 (page 112) to make one folded rose with a gathered extension, using 11" of mauve ruffled-edge ribbon. Gather the last 6" of the ribbon and coil the gathering around the folded center.
4. **Pink rosette**: Refer to diagrams 17a and 17e (page 103) to make one pink rosette, using 6" of 5/8" wide pale pink silk ribbon. Cover the center with seven pearl seed beads.
5. **Lace and gold rosette**: Refer to diagrams 17a and 17e (page 103) to make one rosette, using 4" of 5/8" wide lace. Make a second rosette, using 4" of 1/2" wide gold ribbon. Place the gold rosette on top of the lace rosette and stitch them together. Insert five double-headed gold stamens in the center.
6. **Cream/pink blossom**: Refer to diagrams 25a-25b (page 106) to make one cream four-petal blos-

som, using 9" of 1" wide cream wire-edge ribbon. Refer to diagrams 17a and 17e (page 103) to make one pink rosette, using 6" of 5/8" wide pale pink silk ribbon. Place the pink rosette on top of the cream blossom and stitch them together. Cover the center with seven pink seed beads.

7. Mitered leaves: Refer to diagrams 39a-39d (page 117) to make three mitered leaves, using 3" of olive ruffled-edge ribbon for each leaf.

8. Prairie point leaves: Refer to diagrams 35a-35d (page 113) to make six prairie point leaves, using 2-1/2" of green ombre wire-edge ribbon for each leaf.

9. Pleated fans: Make two pleated fans, using 3" of olive green pleated ribbon for each. Gather tightly across the bottom of each piece of ribbon so it fans out.

Put the composition together on crinoline:
1. Stitch the wine wild rose to the center of the bow.
2. Stitch on the decorative elements in the following order: one fan of pleated ribbon, the double folded rose, the mauve folded rose, the cream blossom, the pink rosette, the lace/gold rosette, the second pleated fan of ribbon, and the leaves.
3. Trim away the excess crinoline and stitch the composition to the front of the shoe (or the base you are using).

Chapter 5
Ribbon Flower Embellishments

Red Purse   Page 61

Flowers on a Ball Gown   Page 67

Scarf Chatelaine   Page 64

Red Purse

A tiny motif of ribbon flowers and leaves in a vintage style embellishes this little red silk purse.

With just a very small piece of luscious silk fabric and the same amount of commercially embroidered black net lace you can make a stunning evening purse like this one. The only ribbonwork on this piece is the rose, three blossoms, and the three leaves. The finished size of the purse is 5-3/4" tall by 5" wide.

My sewing knowledge is somewhat suspect but I believe you will have no trouble putting this purse together. Please feel free to adapt any of the sewing instructions.

You will need:

- 12" x 6" piece red dupioni silk fabric
- 12" x 6" piece embroidered black net lace fabric
- 12" x 6" piece black moiré fabric
- 4-1/2" black ribbon, 1/2" wide
- 3-1/2" red ribbon, 3/8" wide
- 6-3/4" yellow/green ruffled-edge ribbon, 1/4" wide
- 9-3/4" gold ribbon, 1/4" wide
- 48" fancy black and gold trim
- 6 gold seed beads
- Garnet bead
- 33 metallic red seed beads
- 10 red glass dagger beads
- Snap closure

Steps:

Make the flowers and leaves:

1. Rose: The rose is made of two rosettes, one on top of the other. Refer to diagrams 17a and 17d (page 103) to make the bottom rosette from 4-1/2" of black ribbon and the top rosette from 3-1/2" of red ribbon. Note that the red ribbon is folded along its length and pressed before the u-gather pattern is stitched. The fold edge is the outside edge of the red rosette. Stitch the red rosette to the black rosette. Cover the center of the red rosette with six seed beads and a garnet bead.

2. Gold blossoms: Refer to diagrams 25a-25b (page 106) to make three blossoms, using 3-1/4" of

gold ribbon for each blossom. Cover the center of each with one small red metallic bead.

3. Leaves: Refer to diagrams 38a-38e (page 116) to make three half-boat leaves, using 2-1/2" of the yellow/green ruffled-edge ribbon for each.

Prepare the purse:

1. Lining: On the short edges of the black moiré fabric, fold 3/8" to the wrong side and press. Fold the fabric, right sides facing, aligning the two short edges. Sew up the side seams with 1/2" seam allowance. Do not turn inside out.

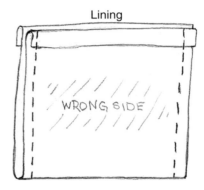

Lining

2. Sew a snap closure to the center of the top inside edge. Set aside.

3. Purse: Lay the lace on top of the red silk, both fabrics right side up. Join the fabrics together by sewing a 1/4" zigzag seam around all four sides of the fabrics. Fold the short ends of the fabrics to the wrong side 1/4" and press. Set aside.

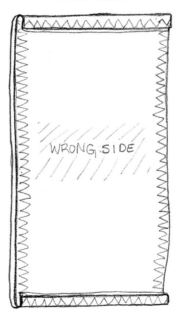

Purse "fabric"

Put the flowers, leaves, and beads on the silk/lace fabric:

1. Referring to the photo and the illustration below for placement, stitch the flowers and leaves to the front of the silk/lace fabric.

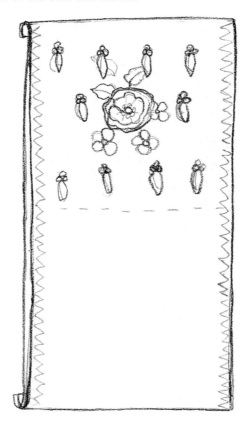

2. Follow the illustration for the beading. The beads are strung on a 7" thread. Go down through all the beads, across the bottom bead and back up through all the beads. Remove the needle from the thread and re-thread both threads through the needle. Stitch the bead dangle to the purse. I made a total of ten dangles with three red seed beads and one dagger bead on each.

Completing the purse:

1. With the embellishing complete, fold the silk/lace fabric in half, right sides facing, and align the short sides. Sew the sides with a 1/4" seam allowance.

2. Stitch the fancy black and gold strap to the inside at each side seam.

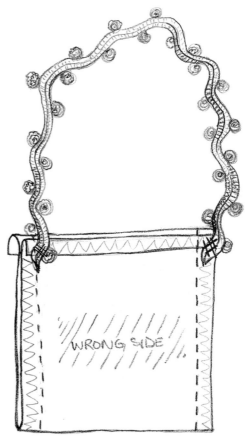

3. Turn the purse right side out.

4. Insert the black lining into the silk/lace purse, aligning the side seams. Stitch the lining to the purse with hidden slipstitches all the way around the top edge of the purse.

Scarf Chatelaine

This elegant scarf chatelaine is embellished with bias-cut silk ribbon roses. Below the scarf are antique sewing tools, an antique German half doll pincushion, and an Edwardian silver chatelaine.

𝒯his scarf with floral embellishments is really my version of a very elegant sewing chatelaine. The actual chatelaine is the detachable flower brooch, with three strings of exquisite beads from which the sewing "tools" are hung. If you don't want to make a scarf you can certainly use a purchased one or just make the chatelaine/brooch for use by itself.

A note about the roses - all of them are made from bias-cut silk ribbon that has been folded in half and pressed flat before being stitched.

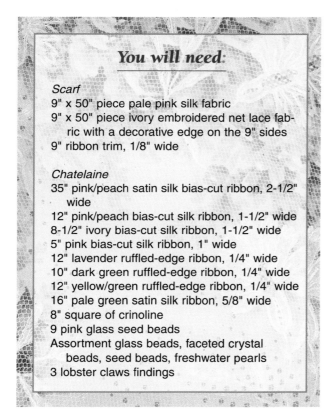

You will need:

Scarf
9" x 50" piece pale pink silk fabric
9" x 50" piece ivory embroidered net lace fabric with a decorative edge on the 9" sides
9" ribbon trim, 1/8" wide

Chatelaine
35" pink/peach satin silk bias-cut ribbon, 2-1/2" wide
12" pink/peach bias-cut silk ribbon, 1-1/2" wide
8-1/2" ivory bias-cut silk ribbon, 1-1/2" wide
5" pink bias-cut silk ribbon, 1" wide
12" lavender ruffled-edge ribbon, 1/4" wide
10" dark green ruffled-edge ribbon, 1/4" wide
12" yellow/green ruffled-edge ribbon, 1/4" wide
16" pale green satin silk ribbon, 5/8" wide
8" square of crinoline
9 pink glass seed beads
Assortment glass beads, faceted crystal beads, seed beads, freshwater pearls
3 lobster claws findings

Steps:

Make the scarf:
1. Stitch a narrow hem on the 9" sides of the silk fabric.
2. Centering the lace fabric over the silk fabric, lay the fabrics right sides facing. Stitch the long sides together. Turn the scarf right sides out.
3. Put the scarf around your neck and mark the spot where you would comfortably wear a brooch. At this spot, on both sides of the scarf, gather across the scarf to a width of 3".

4. Cover the gathering stitches on each side of the scarf with a 4-1/2" length of 1/8" wide ribbon trim.

Make the flowers and leaves:
1. Cabochon rosebud: Refer to Rose #13a in the Combination Rose Guide (page 121). Use 6" of 1-1/2" wide pink/peach silk ribbon folded in half for the rose center. Use 3" of 2-1/2" wide pink/peach silk ribbon folded in half for each of the three rose petals. Overlap the three petals by a third and link them together with stitches at the base of the petals. Wrap these petals around the rose center.

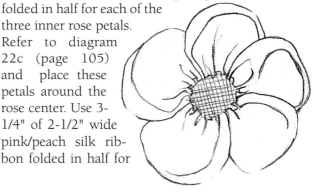

Stitch through all the layers of ribbon to secure. Trim the raw edges and finish by wrapping a 2" piece of pale green satin ribbon over the raw edges at the base of the rose.

2. Large rose: Refer to Rose #14 in the Combination Rose Guide (page 121). Use 6" of 1-1/2" wide pink/peach silk ribbon folded in half for the rose center. Use 3 " of 2-1/2" wide pink/peach silk ribbon folded in half for each of the three inner rose petals. Refer to diagram 22c (page 105) and place these petals around the rose center. Use 3-1/4" of 2-1/2" wide pink/peach silk ribbon folded in half for

Project Tip

To encourage the cabochon rosebud petals to "sit down" after they're attached to the crinoline, take a few hidden stitches under each of the three petals.

each of the five single u-gather outer petals. Cut a 3/4" circle of crinoline and evenly arrange and stitch these five petals around the edge.

Stitch the cabochon rosebud to the center of the five petals.

3. Mini open rose: Refer to Rose #15 in the Combination Rose Guide (page 121). Use 5" of 1" wide pink silk ribbon folded in half for the coiled center. Gather the ribbon to 2" long. On the 8-1/2" length of ivory silk ribbon folded in half, lightly pencil mark the fold edge of the ribbon, leaving 3/4" margin at the ends, and 1-1/2" spacing across the length of the ribbon. Draw up the ruching to about 3/4". Before securing the ruching make sure the petals will fit around the coiled rose center. Finish the rose by wrapping 2" of pale green satin silk ribbon around the stem, so the raw edges of the rose are covered.

4. Lavender rosettes: Refer to diagrams 17a and 17f (page 103) to make three double rosettes, using 4" of lavender ruffled-edge ribbon for each rosette. Gather the ribbon to 1-1/4" long. Coil and tack the gathered ribbon on a 1/2" circle of crinoline. Cover each center with three pink seed beads.

5. Leaves: Refer to diagrams 38a-38d (page 116) to make three half-boat leaves, using 4" of pale green satin ribbon per leaf. Make five small half-boat leaves, using 2-1/4" of yellow/green ruffled-edge ribbon per leaf. Make four small half-boat leaves, using 2-1/4" of dark green ruffled-edge ribbon per leaf.

Put the composition together on crinoline:

1. Using the photo as a placement guide, stitch the flowers and leaves to a 4" square of crinoline. Assemble in the following order: large rose, three pale green leaves, cabochon rosebud, mini rose, small leaves, rosettes. Carefully cut away the excess crinoline and set aside.

2. Use the illustration at right to bead the chatelaine. Thread a milliner's needle with 18" of single thread. Put on each bead starting at the top of the diagram. When you reach the bottom of the string, thread on the lobster claw finding, just as you would a bead. Complete the beading by going back up through all the beads you have strung. You now have two threads coming out of the top of the strand of beads. Re-thread the needle with both strands of thread and stitch the strand of beads under the main rose. Make a total of three strings of beads.

Project Tip

My illustrator, Karen, has a good suggestion for the strings of beads. If you want to wear the chatelaine as a brooch without the silver sewing tools attached, simply loop each string of beads and clip it to itself under the large rose.

Finishing Tip

Finish the chatelaine by gluing a piece of Ultrasuede to the back, so all the crinoline is covered. Add a pin back to the back and pin the chatelaine/ brooch to the scarf.

Flowers for a Ball Gown

Ribbon flowers adorn the neckline of a ball gown.

Detail of ribbonwork flowers on a court gown from the Paris design house, Boué Soeurs. The ribbon flowers are stitched over white net embroidered in silver cord. The gown was worn by Mrs. George Henry O'Neil, for presentation before King George V in June, 1928. The Metropolitan Museum of Art, Gift of Mrs. George Henry O'Neil, 1968. (CI.68.48) Photograph by Sheldan Collins. Photograph copyright 1986 The Metropolitan Museum of Art.

Heirloom Ribbonwork

During the mid to late 1920s it was not uncommon to embellish an evening gown with ribbonwork. Dressmakers either made the flowers themselves or used beautiful pre-made floral motifs that were exported from France. The two gowns shown on these pages are from the famous Paris design house Boué Soeurs, which was renowned for its use of ribbonwork.

With ribbonwork enjoying a revival I was inspired to create some ribbon flowers to embellish the neckline of the cream ball gown, shown on page 67. The flowers presented are not difficult to make and are well worth your time and effort.

You will need:

Note: The supplies given are for the neckline of the ball gown I used. Please adjust the supplies to suit your gown.

22" green looped ribbon trim
18" pink/peach bias-cut silk ribbon, 1-1/2" wide
27" pink/peach satin silk bias-cut ribbon, 2-1/2" wide
14-1/2" ivory bias-cut silk ribbon, 1-1/2" wide
9" ivory satin silk bias-cut ribbon, 2-1/2" wide
15" pink bias-cut silk ribbon, 1" wide
17" pink bias-cut silk ribbon, 1-1/2" wide
36" cream ruffled-edge ribbon, 1" wide
25-1/2" blue/gold ribbed ribbon, 1/2" wide
31-1/2" blue/green ruffled-edge ribbon, 1/4" wide
20-1/4" green ruffled-edge ribbon, 1/4" wide
4-1/2" yellow/green ruffled-edge ribbon, 1/4" wide
11-1/4" green ruffled-gold-edge ribbon, 1/4" wide
6 smoke/blue crystal beads
29 yellow frosted seed beads
48 gold double-headed stamens
8" x 12" piece of crinoline

This logo and gown are part of an advertisement for Boué Soeurs lace gowns in the June 1927 issue of World Traveler *magazine. Note the ribbon rose sprays on the front of the gown and at the bow.*

ROBES, MANTEAUX & LINGERIE
BOUÉ SŒURS
9, RUE DE LA PAIX, PARIS
SAN FRANCISCO
St. Francis Hotel
PALM BEACH
North Lake Trail
NEW YORK
13 West 56th Street

Steps:

Make the flowers and leaves:

1. Peach roses: Refer to Rose #13a in the Combination Rose Guide (page 100) and make three large peach roses, using 6" of 1-1/2" wide pink/peach silk ribbon folded in half for each center. Use 3" of 2-1/2" wide pink/peach silk ribbon folded in half for each of the three petals in each rose. Overlap and stitch the petals together and wrap around the coiled rose center as shown.

2. Ivory rose: Refer to Rose #13b in the Combination Rose Guide (page 100) to make one ivory rose. Although this rose is very similar to the pink roses above, its construction is like the rolled-edge cabochon roses. Use 6" of 1-1/2" wide ivory silk ribbon folded in half for the center. Use 3" of 2-1/2" wide ivory folded in half for each of the three petals. Stitch the coiled center to a 3/4" circle of crinoline. Refer to diagram 22c (page 105) and stitch each petal over the coiled center.

3. Miniature roses: Refer to Rose #15 in the Combination Rose Guide (page 121) to make three mini open roses. Use 5" of 1" wide pink silk ribbon folded in half for each of the three coiled centers. Gather the ribbon to 2" long. Use 8-1/2" of 1-1/2" wide pink silk ribbon folded in half for two sets of the outer petals and ivory for the third set of petals. With a pencil, lightly mark the fold edge of the ribbon, leaving 3/4" margin at the ends and 1-1/2" spacing across the length of the ribbon (like the blossoms in the Brown Brooch project, page 38). Draw up the ruching to about 3/4". Before securing the ruching make sure the petals will fit around the coiled rose center.

4. Cream folded roses: Refer to diagrams 32a-32f (page 111) to make four folded roses, using 9" of cream ruffled-edge ribbon for each rose.

5. Blue/gold rosettes: Refer to diagrams 17a and 17d (page 103) to make six large rosettes, using 4-1/4" of blue/gold ribbed ribbon for each rosette. Insert eight double-headed gold stamens in each center and one crystal bead.

6. Small blue/green rosettes: Refer to diagrams 17a and 17d (page 103) to make five small rosettes, using 2-1/2" of blue/green ruffled ribbon for each. Cover the center of each with three yellow seed beads.

7. Double spiral blue/green rosettes: Refer to diagrams 17a and 17f (page 103) to make two double spiral rosettes, using 4" of blue/green ruf-fled ribbon for each. Gather to a length of 1-1/4". Stitch the gathered ribbon to the center of a 3/4" circle of crinoline, in a spiral. Cover each center with three yellow seed beads.

8. Triple spiral blue/green rosettes: Refer to diagram 17a and 17g (page 103) to make two triple spiral rosettes, using 5-1/4" of blue/green ruffled ribbon for each. Gather to a length of 2-1/4". Stitch the gathered ribbon to the center of a 3/4" circle of crinoline, in a spiral. Cover each center with four yellow seed beads.

9. Leaves: Refer to diagrams 38a-38e (page 116) to make nine green half-boat leaves, using 2-1/4" of 1/4" wide green ruffled-edge ribbon for each. Make another two half-boat leaves, using 2-1/4" of the yellow/green ruffled-edge ribbon for each. Make five more half-boat leaves, using 2-1/4" of the 1/4" wide ruffled-gold-edge green ribbon for each leaf.

Put the composition together on crinoline:

1. Refer to the photo for placement of the flowers and leaves.

2. With a pencil, trace the shape of the neckline on the crinoline.

3. Stitch the 22" length of green loop ribbon trim to the crinoline along the traced neckline.

4. Stitch the ivory rose and the three peach silk roses to the center of the composition. Stitch the two cream folded roses are stitched beside these. Follow this with the blue/gold rosettes, two more cream folded roses, some leaves, the mini roses and the nine blue/green rosettes. Stitch the remaining leaves around and under the flowers as needed.

5. Carefully trim away the excess crinoline and stitch the composition to the neckline of the ball gown.

Chapter 6
Ribbonwork in Your Home

Moon Cottage Album Page 72

Footstool with Cabochon Roses Page 74

Roses on the Wing Page 82

Lavender-Filled Sachet Page 76

Parasol With Flowers Page 79

Moon Cottage Album

This green covered album with exquisite French jacquard ribbons is the easiest project in the whole book. With just a few folds of some fabric and the addition of some ribbons you will have the album covered and the embellishing complete in no time at all. Look again at the photo and notice the small cream album with the pale green bow. This tiny album has a silk print surrounded by looped trim as the focal point with a ribbon bow embellishing the spine. A quick and lovely gift, don't you think?

The nostalgic silk print of the cottage beside a moonlit lake was the inspiration for the green album and I am sure that you will have many ideas for your own albums too. The silk prints are lovely used as is or can be embellished with silk ribbon embroidery, beads, and miniature ribbon flowers before being attached to the album. Use this project as a starting point for embellishing albums on a more lavish scale. Add ribbon flowers, buttons, charms, and even decorative stitches between the joined ribbons. Also realize that any ribbon flower composition in this book could be adapted and added to the album cover.

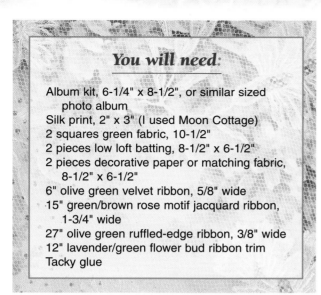

You will need:

Album kit, 6-1/4" x 8-1/2", or similar sized
  photo album
Silk print, 2" x 3" (I used Moon Cottage)
2 squares green fabric, 10-1/2"
2 pieces low loft batting, 8-1/2" x 6-1/2"
2 pieces decorative paper or matching fabric,
  8-1/2" x 6-1/2"
6" olive green velvet ribbon, 5/8" wide
15" green/brown rose motif jacquard ribbon,
  1-3/4" wide
27" olive green ruffled-edge ribbon, 3/8" wide
12" lavender/green flower bud ribbon trim
Tacky glue

Steps:

Cover the album:

1. For the album kit, follow the manufacturer's instructions for putting the bindings together. If you are covering a three-ring binder or other photo album, use your favorite method of covering.

2. The following suggestions are merely that - suggestions. Lightly glue one piece of batting to the front cover and the other piece of batting to the back cover. Place the fabric over the batting and trim off the excess fabric, leaving a 1-1/4" margin around all four sides. Fold each of the long ends of fabric in first, followed by the short ends. Carefully trim down the excess fabric that may form in the corners. Tuck in the corners and secure with glue. Set aside. The back sides of these covers will be finished later.

Embellish the cover:

1. Refer to the photo for placement. Lightly apply tacky glue to the ribbons and adhere them to the cover, moving from the cor-  ners toward the center. Butt the ribbons tightly together or overlap very slightly. Start with the olive velvet ribbon, followed by the jacquard rose motif ribbon, and the green ruffled-edge ribbon. Cover the join between the jacquard and the velvet ribbon with the flower bud trim. Bring the excess of

each ribbon to the back of the cover and firmly glue it in place.

2. Cut a small piece of batting to fit the image area of the silk print. Place this on the back of the silk print. Trim the edges of the silk print to 1/4", turn the raw edges to the back and over the batting, and very carefully press the edges flat. Apply tacky glue to the edges on the back of the silk print and gently adhere the green ruffled-edge ribbon to the silk print.

3. Glue the print once more around the edges and attach it to the center of the album.

4. Cut two small flower bud ribbon motifs (seal the ends with fabric sealer) and glue one to each side of the silk print.

Finish the album:

1. Finish the album covers by gluing a piece of decorative paper (or matching fabric), to the back of the cover about 1/2" from the edges. Decorate the edges with narrow ribbon trim, especially if using fabric and the raw edges aren't folded under.

Project Tip

While there are no ribbon flowers to make for this project, they could certainly be added at a later time. Thread-sculpted folded roses with a few curved leaves would be very attractive at each edge of the silk print or in the corners of the cover.

Footstool With
Cabochon Roses

Cabochon roses were the staple of 1920s ribbonwork - gracing lingerie, vanity items, and dresses. Still a very popular rose today, I have incorporated the cabochon rose in a composition suitable for many uses and especially for the footstool shown, which was purchased in a craft shop and later re-covered. You could recycle any footstool you have at home, or even do something totally different with the flower composition. Perhaps you might use the flowers in a curtain tieback, or on a cushion, or even a photo album. Whatever base you choose will be perfect!

A note about the ribbons: Look at the cabochon roses - the cinnamon/raspberry rose is made with new ribbon while the two peach roses (and three rosebuds) were made with vintage French ribbon. Whether you use vintage or new ribbons, the roses will be lovely. All the other elements in the composition were made with new ribbons.

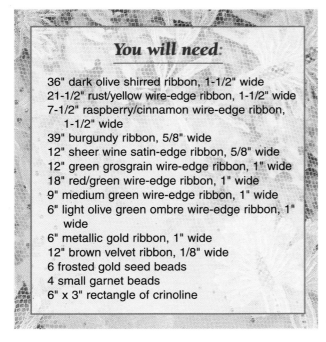

You will need:

36" dark olive shirred ribbon, 1-1/2" wide
21-1/2" rust/yellow wire-edge ribbon, 1-1/2" wide
7-1/2" raspberry/cinnamon wire-edge ribbon, 1-1/2" wide
39" burgundy ribbon, 5/8" wide
12" sheer wine satin-edge ribbon, 5/8" wide
12" green grosgrain wire-edge ribbon, 1" wide
18" red/green wire-edge ribbon, 1" wide
9" medium green wire-edge ribbon, 1" wide
6" light olive green ombre wire-edge ribbon, 1" wide
6" metallic gold ribbon, 1" wide
12" brown velvet ribbon, 1/8" wide
6 frosted gold seed beads
4 small garnet beads
6" x 3" rectangle of crinoline

Steps:

Make the bow:
1. This bow is made in two sections with three loops on each half of the bow. It is similar in construction to the five loop bow, diagram 14 (page 100). Cut the dark olive shirred ribbon into two 18" pieces. On each piece measure and pin 8" from one end, measure another 6" from this point, and another 4" to the end of the ribbon. Make a large loop from the 8" section, a medium loop from the 6" section, and a small loop from the 4" section. Secure these loops with stitches. Both bow halves will be stitched to the crinoline.

Make the flowers and leaves:
1. Roses: Refer to Rose #9 in the Combination Rose Guide (page 120) and make three roses. For each center, use 9" of 5/8" wide burgundy ribbon. For the three outer petals on two roses use 2-1/2" of rust/yellow ribbon for each petal and raspberry/cinnamon ribbon for the petals on the third rose.
2. Rosebuds: Make three cabochon buds. Use 2" of 5/8" wide burgundy for each center. Fold the burgundy ribbon across itself (similar to a prairie point leaf) and gather across the bottom. Refer to diagrams 22a-22b (page 105) to make three cabochon rolled edge petals, using 2-1/2" rust/yellow ribbon for each petal. Wrap one petal around one bud center. Finish each bud by wrapping a 1-1/4" piece of 1" wide red/green ribbon around the base.
3. Burgundy blossom: Refer to diagrams 25a-25b (page 106) to make a four-petal blossom, using 6" of 5/8" wide burgundy ribbon for each. Cover the center with six frosted gold seed beads.
4. Wine rosettes: Refer to diagrams 20a-20c (page 104) to make four rosettes, using 3" of sheer satin-edge wine ribbon folded in half lengthwise for each. Cover each center with one garnet bead.
5. Leaves: Refer to diagrams 39a-39d (page 117) to make 15 mitered green leaves, using 3" of 1" wide assorted green wire-edge ribbons for each. Make four green grosgrain leaves, four red/green leaves, three medium green leaves, two light olive green ombre leaves, and two gold leaves.

Put the composition together on crinoline:
1. Refer to the photo for placement and stitch to the crinoline as follows:
Bow halves, three roses on top of the bow, some leaves around and under the roses, burgundy blossom to the right of the roses.
2. Twist some brown velvet ribbon around the bow loops to resemble vines. Stitch the three rosebuds near the folds of the bow. Stitch the wine rosettes around the roses and leaves.
3. Carefully trim away the excess crinoline.
4. Stitch the flower composition to the footstool or the base of your choice.

Lavender-Filled Sachet

Antique trims and ribbon flowers were common embellishments on ladies vanity items during the early part of the 1900s. This new sachet, with ribbon flowers in a basket, is filled with lavender and would be lovely on a dresser as a resting place for brooches.

What could be finer for your dressing table or vanity than this fragrant, lavender-filled sachet? It's easy to make and would be a lovely gift for a treasured friend. Or, use it as a brooch pillow as was done in the early years of the 20th century, and decorate it with ribbons, flowers, trims, and tassels.

You will need:

Plum velvet fabric, 6" square
Tulle or plain net lace, 2 6" squares
18" gold sheer ribbon, 1-1/2" wide
18" plum sheer ribbon, 1-1/2" wide
3" metallic lace ribbon, 1-5/8" wide
8-1/2" gold braid, 1/4" wide
16" raspberry/yellow ombre wire-edge ribbon, 1" wide
7" raspberry/cinnamon wire-edge ribbon, 5/8" wide
2" purple ribbon, 5/8" wide
6" lavender ribbon, 1" wide
5" plum ribbon, 3/8" wide
8" white gold-edge ribbon, 1/4" wide
10" olive green ruffled-edge ribbon, 1/2" wide
9" pale green ribbon, 1/2" wide
6 double-headed olive green stamens
4 metallic gold tassels, 1-1/4"
8 glass leaf beads
100 frosted gold seed beads
12 small metallic gold or pearl beads
4" square of crinoline
Cup dried lavender

Steps

1. Cut the two sheer ribbons in six 6" lengths and weave the pieces together in a basket weave style. Baste the woven ribbons edges so the ribbons stay together while the sachet is under construction.

2. Pin the woven ribbon square on top of the tulle or lace squares. Sew these layers together by stitching around the four sides, 1/4" from the edge of the woven ribbons. Remove the temporary basting stitches.

3. Position the four metallic gold tassels in the corners on top of the woven ribbons and stitch the tassel cords in place.

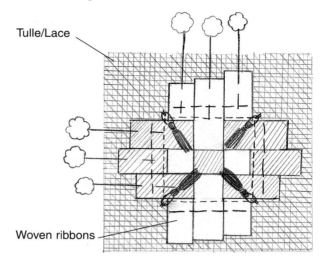

Tulle/Lace

Woven ribbons

4. Lay the 6" square of velvet on top of the woven ribbons with right sides facing. Machine stitch or hand sew around three sides of the square, catching the edge of the woven ribbon in the seam.
Trim the edges and corners from the fabric and turn the sachet right side out. The woven ribbon side is the front.

5. Make eight bead tassels as shown.

6. Sew two bead tassels to each corner, next to the metallic gold tassel. Set aside the sachet.

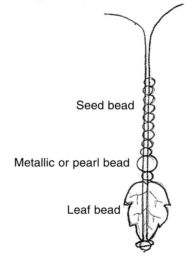

Seed bead

Metallic or pearl bead

Leaf bead

Make the ribbon basket:

1. Trim the edges of the metallic lace ribbon to form a "boat" shape. Tack the two raw edges and the bottom edge of the lace to the 4" piece of crinoline.

2. Evenly arrange the gold braid for the basket handle so it covers the raw edges of the basket base and makes a pleasing handle shape. Turn under the raw edges of the trim and stitch the handle in place. The completed basket can measure between 2" to 3" tall.

Make the flowers and leaves:

1. Folded roses: Refer to diagrams 32a-3f (page 111) to make three folded roses, using 9" of raspberry/yellow ribbon for one rose and 7" for the second rose. Use 7" of raspberry/cinnamon ribbon for the third rose.

2. Purple rose: Refer to Rose #11 in the Combination Rose Guide (page 120). Use 2" of purple ribbon for the center and simply roll it up into a tube. Use 6" of lavender ribbon, folded up 2/3. Wrap this double ruffle around the purple center and secure with stitches.

3. Plum blossom: Refer to diagrams 25a-25b (page 106) to make a four-petal blossom, using 5" of plum ribbon. Wrap the gathered ribbon petals around six double-headed green stamens.

4. White rosettes: Refer to diagrams 17a and 17d (page 103) to make four rosettes, using 2" of white gold-edge ribbon for each. Cover the center with one small metallic bead or small pearl bead.

5. Leaves: Refer to diagrams 38a-38d (page 116) to make four half-boat leaves, using 2-1/2" of the olive ruffled-edge ribbon for each. Make another three leaves, using 3" of green ribbon for each.

Put the composition together on crinoline:

1. Refer to the photo and stitch in this order: main three roses, leaves around and under the roses, the large purple rose, the plum blossom, and the rosettes around the roses and leaves.
2. Trim the excess crinoline from the composition and stitch the basket of flowers to the sachet front.

Finish the sachet:

1. Fill the sachet with as much lavender as desired.
2. Fold in the raw edges of the opening and stitch closed with hidden slipstitches.

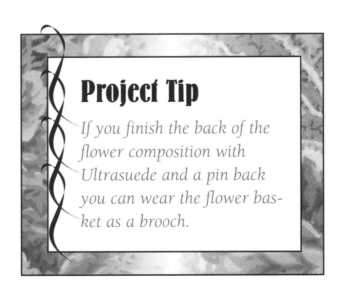

Project Tip

If you finish the back of the flower composition with Ultrasuede and a pin back you can wear the flower basket as a brooch.

Parasol With Flowers

Ribbon roses and blossoms are gathered into a lace parasol and framed in an antique oval frame with a domed glass to protect the flowers.

A sampler of ribbon roses, flowers, and leaves are casually arranged in a lace parasol. This project was taught at one of my Summer Retreats and while not difficult to do, it does involve a lot of steps. You'll make the parasol first then make all the flowers. The height of this parasol composition is 11" and the width is 6-1/2", making it ideal for framing. It also looks very good when used to embellish a cushion.

Keep this project for a rainy weekend!

You will need:

5" peach grosgrain ribbon, 3" wide
9" fine cream lace, 5" wide
6" beige/gold ribbed ribbon, 7/16" wide
2" peach/cream bow ribbon, 3/8" wide
10" yellow wire-edge grosgrain ribbon, 1" wide
30" peach/cream wire-edge ribbon, 1" wide
10" gold wire-edge ribbon, 1" wide
24" cinnamon/raspberry wire-edge ribbon, 1" wide
34" cream wire-edge ribbon, 1" wide
32" purple bias-cut silk ribbon, 5/8" wide
10" yellow bias-cut silk ribbon, 7/16" wide
15" pink ruffled-edge ribbon, 5/8" wide
12" thin green cord (or 32-gauge thread-covered wire)
6" blue/purple ruffled-edge ribbon, 1/4" wide
6-3/4" pink/lavender ruffled-edge ribbon, 1/4" wide
40" olive ombre wire-edge ribbon, 1" wide
9" hunter green wire-edge ribbon, 1" wide
8" sheer lime green wire-edge ribbon, 1-1/2" wide
10" lime green wire-edge ribbon, 1" wide
5 gold double-headed stamens
Small gold bead
3 yellow seed beads
6 pearl seed beads
12" x 7" piece of crinoline
Mauve glass button, 3/4" diameter

Steps:

Make the parasol:

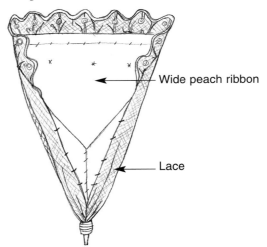

Wide peach ribbon

Lace

1. Use the photo and the illustration for guidance. The parasol is an elongated triangle shape with a liner of peach ribbon and an overlay of gathered lace. Fold the raw edge of the wide peach ribbon down at the top 1/8" and sew a very narrow hem. Fold the bottom corners in to form a point and tack the folds in place.

2. Tightly gather 9" of lace across the bottom. Pin the gathered end to the base of the parasol, right side up. Arrange the gathers at the point and stitch the lace to the ribbon. Wrap your thread around this point once or twice and secure the thread. Fold in the edges of the lace and tack them to the back of the ribbon triangle. Arrange the lace at the top into folds in the front of the parasol and secure these folds with five pearl seed beads anywhere near the top.

3. Make a point for the bottom of the parasol with a 1" piece of beige/gold ribbed ribbon. Stitch it in the back of the parasol under the lace point.

4. Cover the lace point on the front with 2" of peach/cream bow trim.

5. Sew the remaining pearl seed bead to the bow trim.

6. Stitch the parasol to the bottom of a 12" x 7" piece of crinoline.

7. Refer to diagram 3 (page 97) to make a ribbon handle for the parasol. Center 5" of beige/gold ribbed ribbon over the parasol, and align it with the bottom point. Fold over the end of the ribbon and stitch it in place. Gently twist the ribbon as you sew it to the crinoline to form the handle. The parasol, plus handle, should measure 11" in height.

Make the flowers and leaves:

1. Coiled rose: Refer to diagrams 18a-18c (page 103) to make one yellow coiled rose, using 10" of yellow wire-edge grosgrain ribbon.

2. Folded rose: Refer to diagrams 32a-32f (page 111) to make one folded rose, using 10" of peach/cream wire-edge ribbon.

3. Pinch petal rose: Refer to diagrams 31a-31g (page 110) to make one pinch petal rose, using 10" of gold wire-edge ribbon. The petals are the top pinched style. Each petal uses 2" of ribbon. Use five double headed stamens and a small gold bead for the center.

4. Tea rose: Refer to Rose #7 in the Combination Rose Guide (page 119) to make one tea rose, using 10" of cinnamon/raspberry tea rose ribbon for the center and 14" for the seven outer petals. Each petal uses 2" of ribbon.

5. Cabbage roses: Refer to Rose #4 in the Combination Rose Guide (page 119) to make two cabbage roses, using 10" of peach/cream ribbon for the center of each. Use 7" of cream ribbon for the first row of petals and 10" of cream ribbon for the second row of petals. Stagger the second row of petals when stitching them to the first row of petals.

6. Hydrangea blossoms: Refer to diagrams 25a-25b (page 106) to make five four-petal u-gather hydrangea blossoms, using 6-1/4" of purple bias-cut silk ribbon for each blossom. Refer to diagram 4 (page 97) to make an overhand knot from 2" of yellow bias-cut silk ribbon. Wrap the gathered ribbon petals around the overhand knot.

7. Bell flowers: Refer to diagram 16h (page 102) to make six bell flowers, using 2-1/2" of the ruffled-edge pink ribbon for each flower and 2" of thin green cord for each of the stems.

8. Mini pansies: Refer to diagrams 23a and 23c (page 105) to make the back petals for the three faux mini pansies, using 2" of blue/lavender ruffled-edge ribbon for each. Refer to diagrams 17a and 17d (page 103) to make the pansy fronts, using 2-1/4" of the pink/lavender ruffled-edge ribbon for each. Stitch the front petals over the back petals. Finish each center with a yellow seed bead.

9. Boat leaves: Refer to diagrams 37a-37d (page 115) to make eight boat leaves, using 5" of olive wire-edge ribbon for each. Alternate the ombre edge so some of the leaf points are light and others are dark.

10. Mitered leaves: Refer to diagrams 39a-39d (page 117) to make three mitered leaves, using 3" of hunter green wire-edge ribbon for each.

11. Prairie point leaves: Refer to diagrams 35a-35d (page 113) to make two large prairie point leaves, using 4" of 1-1/2" wide sheer lime green wire-edge ribbon for each. Make four small prairie point leaves, using 2-1/2" of 1" wide lime green wire-edge ribbon for each.

Put the composition together on crinoline:

1. Refer to the photo for placement. Tack the two cream cabbage roses to the crinoline, follow with the gold rose, the cinnamon/raspberry rose, the yellow rose, and the small peach rose. Add the large leaves around the sides and top. Add the hydrangea blossoms, the three mini pansies and the six pink bell flowers.

2. Fill in with the remaining leaves. When all the elements are in place, secure them with a few more stitches to the crinoline.

3. Sew the glass button to the top of the handle.

4. Cut away the excess crinoline and your flower/parasol composition is ready to be stitched to a cushion or to be framed.

Roses
on the
Wing

This very quick project of ribbon roses in a unique holder makes a lovely gift.

As you may have realized by now, ribbon-work is not usually done in a hurry. It is something that warrants taking your time. First, so that you enjoy the process and second, so that your best effort is put into the project.

However, you may also have realized that some elements of ribbonwork can go very quickly. And one of those elements is making folded roses - which is why you see a lot of them in the craft books. The key to making beautiful and very versatile folded roses is to experiment with many styles of ribbon, widths, lengths, etc. Don't let the standard folded rose become boring!

The project shown uses bias-cut silk ribbons for the roses and can be completed in under an hour, depending on how many roses you make and how many tea breaks you take!

I've hung my roses from a decorative bird holder in my kitchen. Where will you put your roses?

You will need:

Holder - 3 " tall, cone shape (paper, metal, fabric)
30" dusty pink bias-cut silk ribbon, 1-1/2" wide
30" pale pink bias-cut silk ribbon, 1-1/2" wide
30" pink bias-cut silk ribbon, 1-1/2" wide
2 yds. olive green bias-cut silk ribbon, 1" wide
8" of 20-gauge thread-covered wire
Floral tape
Floral foam
Hot glue

Steps:

Make the roses and loops:

1. Roses: Refer to diagrams 32a-32f (page 111) to make six folded roses, using 15" of 1-1/2" bias-cut silk ribbon for each (two roses of each color). Do not trim the excess ribbon at the base of these roses. Divide the roses into two groups so there is one of each color in each group. Stitch these three roses together at their base and glue them to a 4" piece of wire. Set aside until the loops are made.

2. Loops: Refer to diagram 12 (page 100) to make two sets of two-loop bows with streamers. Use 36" of the olive green bias-cut silk ribbon for each set. Stitch a set of loops to each group of roses. Cover the stem wire with floral tape.

Arrange the flowers:

1. With some hot glue, secure the floral foam in the holder.
2. Push the rose "picks" into the foam, arrange the bows to your satisfaction, and enjoy these lovely flowers.

Chapter 7
Flowers to Grow

Spring Bulbs   *Page 85*

Magnolias and Berries   *Page 92*

Wild Rose Posy   *Page 94*

Spring Bulbs - Tulips, Jonquils, and Daffodils

I have several fond memories of spring bulbs. One is of my visit to Floriade in Canberra, which is the most spectacular display of spring bulbs in Australia. The gardens are a sea full of colorful tulips, daffodils, jonquils, and hyacinths, many of which are under-planted with pansies. This is an absolute feast for the eyes.

Another spring bulb memory is from my childhood. While growing up in Australia my sister and I always enjoyed the gardens at my grandfather's farm where we especially loved picking the jonquils and daffodils that grew in huge drifts on the cliffs that fell down to the sea. I can still smell that exquisite jonquil fragrance.

And now that I have been suitably inspired by the real flowers, I thought it would be a good idea to try and re-create them in ribbon. So here they are - ready for you to try.

Suitable containers for these ribbon spring bulbs are baskets, pots, wooden buckets, and glass vases and jars. For the basket and pots shown in the photo, use Styrofoam to fill the container so the wires can simply be pushed into it. If using clear glass, some glass marbles in the base of the vase will help to stabilize the flowers.

Enjoy springtime any time of the year with these tulips, jonquils, and daffodils made from ribbons.

Cream Jonquils

You will need:

Note: This supply list is for one stem of jonquils with narrow leaf only.

65" cream wire-edge ribbon, 1" wide
11-1/4" peach (or yellow, or orange) ribbon, 5/8" wide
15 yellow double-headed stamens
5 green double-headed stamen
36" of 32-gauge thread-covered wire
10" of 18-gauge wire
27" olive green bias-cut silk ribbon, 1" wide
18" olive green ombre wire-edge ribbon, 1" wide
10" of 22-gauge thread-covered wire
Green floral tape
Hot glue

Steps:

1. Stamen stems: Each stem of jonquils has five individual florets. Each floret has stamens, a trumpet, and six petals. Prepare the five stamen stems, using one green and three yellow stamens and a 3" piece of 32-gauge wire for each.

2. Trumpets: Refer to diagrams 16a-16b (page 101) to make five trumpets, using 2-1/4" of peach ribbon for each. Insert the stemmed stamens into the tube and gather the base of the tube.

3. Pull the tube gathering very tightly and secure with stitches going through the stamen stems. A dot of glue where the trumpet and stamens come together helps stabilize the stem. Set aside.

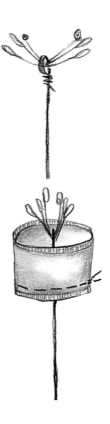

4. Petals: Refer to diagrams 24a-24b (page 106) to make ten sets of the three-petal u-gathers, using 6-1/2" of cream ribbon for each set of petals. Gather tightly and join one set of petals in a ring. Glue this ring of petals to the base of a trumpet. Repeat for all five florets.

5. Offset the second set of petals below the first set and glue in place. Repeat for all five florets.

6. Cover the raw edges of the petals and the stem with floral tape or bias-cut silk ribbon. Style the petals by pinching the top in a point.

7. When all the florets are made, glue all five to the top of a 10" piece of 18-gauge wire.

8. Stem tube cover: Refer to diagrams 16a-16b and 16f (page 101) to make a 6" stem tube to cover the stem, using 27" of olive green bias-cut silk ribbon.

9. Leaf: Jonquil leaves are usually long and narrow. Fold the 18" length of the 1" wide green wire-edge ribbon in half and follow Steps 8, 9, and 10 in the Tulip leaf instructions, page 91.

Yellow Daffodil

Steps:

1. Stamens: Prepare the yellow and green stamens as you did for the jonquils but with 12" of 18-gauge wire.

2. Trumpet: The daffodil's trumpet uses 4-1/2" of 1-1/2" wide yellow/cream wire-edge ribbon. Refer to Steps 2 and 3 in the Jonquil instructions. The stamens will stand up higher than they do in the jonquils.

3. Petals: Refer to diagrams 17a-17b (page 103) to make six single u-gather petals, using 4" of 1-1/2" wide yellow/cream for each petal. Gather each petal tightly.

4. Evenly arrange three yellow petals around the base of the trumpet and stitch or hot glue them to the base of the trumpet. Glue or stitch the remaining three yellow petals under and in between the first yellow petals.

5. Cover the raw edges of the flower petals by wrapping them with 3" of olive green bias-cut silk ribbon.

6. Stem cover: Refer to diagrams 16a-16b and 16f (page 101) to make a stem cover with 9" of olive green bias-cut silk ribbon. Glue or stitch the top of the stem tube to the base of the flower.

7. Style the daffodil petals by pinching the tops into a point.

8. Leaf: Daffodil leaves are usually long and narrow. Fold 18" of the 1" wide green wire-edge ribbon in half and follow Steps 8, 9, and 10 in the Tulip leaf instructions on page 91.

Cream Daffodil

You will need:

Note: This supply list is for one flower and leaf.

24" cream wire-edge ribbon, 1-1/2" wide
4" yellow/orange ombre wire-edge ribbon, 1"
  wide
3 yellow double-headed stamens
1 green double-headed stamen
10" of 18-gauge thread-covered wire
12" olive green bias-cut silk ribbon, 1" wide
18" green wire-edge ribbon, 1" wide
10" of 22-gauge wire
Hot glue
Floral tape

Project Tips

* Use a wide variety of reds, yellows, and pinks for the tulips.
* Vary the height of each flower stem and leaf.
* If you have difficulty using the 18-gauge wire when stemming the stamens, use 22-gauge instead.

Steps:

This cream daffodil is a slight variation of the yellow daffodil and the jonquil. Refer to the jonquil figures for guidance.

1. Stamens: Use yellow and green stamens and the 18-gauge wire to make a stamen stem.

2. Trumpet: The trumpet uses 4" of yellow/orange ribbon. Refer to Step 2 in the Yellow Daffodil.

3. Petals: Refer to diagrams 35a-35d (page 113) to make six petals, using 4" of cream ribbon for each petal. Glue three petals to the base of the trumpet and another three petals, offset and just under these.

4. Stem cover: Refer to Step 6 in the Yellow Daffodil.

5. Leaf: Daffodil leaves are usually long and narrow. Fold 18" of the 1" wide green wire-edge ribbon in half and follow Steps 8, 9, and 10 in the Tulip leaf instructions on page 91.

Red Tulip

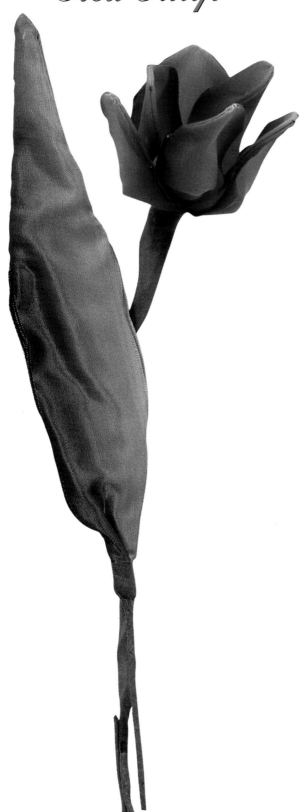

Steps

1. Stamens: The tulip has a stamen center surrounded by six arched petals. Prepare three black stamens as illustrated, using the 18-gauge wire.

2. Petals: Make six petals using 5" of red wire-edge ribbon for each petal. Begin stitching the arched stitch pattern 3/4" from the top fold.

3. When the stitch pattern is complete, turn the ribbon inside out and press

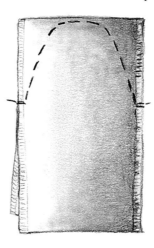

flat. Gather across the bottom of the petal and pull tightly.

4. Stitch the first petal to the stamens.

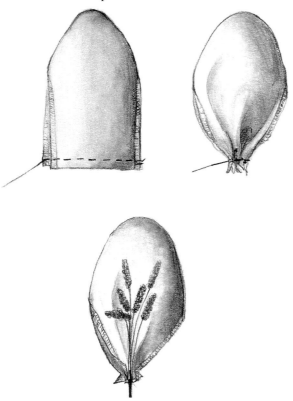

5. Arrange two more petals evenly around the stamens and glue in place. This helps stabilize the stamens on the stem. Glue the remaining three petals under the first row of petals so they peek out between the petals in the first row.

6. Cover the raw edges of the petals and the stem with floral tape or wrap with green bias-cut silk ribbon.

7. Tube stem cover: Refer to diagrams 16a-16b and 16f (page 101) to make a tube stem cover, using 8" of olive green bias-cut silk ribbon. Slip it over the stem and glue/stitch it as close to the base of the petals as possible.

8. Wide leaf: Make a wide tulip leaf using 18" of olive green ombre ribbon and 10" of 22-gauge wire. Fold the ribbon in half and stitch the pattern shown. Start stitching 2" down from the fold.

9. Turn the ribbon right side out and press flat. Insert the wire into the cavity and secure with a dot of glue at the raw edge of the ribbon.

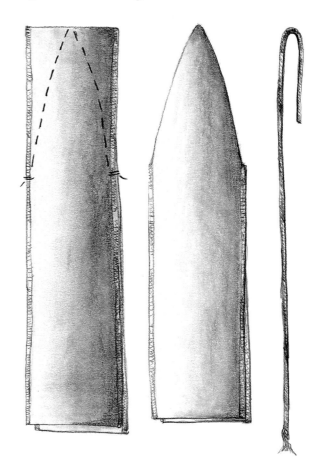

10. Fold the base of the ribbon on itself and secure with floral tape.

Magnolias and Berries

Set against a rustic door, this elegant silver cone with its three magnolias and berry sprays is suitable for display year round.

The simple elegance of these cream magnolias, plum-colored berries, and pine boughs is not to be underestimated. Displays like this are wonderful for your front door at Christmas time and even for year round display in your home. Make several - one to give and one to keep!

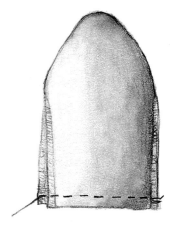

You will need:

6" container for holding flowers (metal, paper, or fabric cone) with handle
45" cream wire-edge ribbon, 1-1/2" wide
90" cream wire-edge ribbon, 1-1/2" or 2" wide
9" pale green wire-edge ribbon, 1-3/4" wide
1 yd. plum wire-edge ribbon, 1" wide
5 artificial pine bough branches, each about 9" long
9" of 20-gauge thread-covered wire
36" of 22-gauge thread-covered wire
28" of 32-gauge thread-covered wire
Small bag of fiberfill or cotton balls
Brown floral tape
Green floral tape
Floral foam
Hot glue
Tacky glue

3. On each flower, stitch a small petal to the pod center, followed by the other two small petals.
4. Stitch the five larger petals around the small petals.
5. Cover the raw edges of the petals with green floral tape, and continue on down the wire stem.

Make the berries:
1. Refer to diagrams 16a-16e (page 101) to make 14 small berries, using 2-1/2" of 1" wide plum ribbon and 2" of 32-gauge wire for each berry.
2. Wrap each berry stem with brown floral tape.
3. Make two berry sprays. Each berry spray has seven berries. With brown floral tape, tape one berry to the top of an 18" piece of 22-gauge wire. Add six more berries, spaced about 1" apart, and continue down the stem in a random manner.

Arrange the composition in the container:
1. Fill the inside of the container with floral foam.
2. Push the pine bough stems, in a fan shape, into the foam.
3. Add the three magnolias near the center and then the berry sprays off to the sides.

Steps:

Make three magnolias:
1. Pod center: Refer to diagrams 16a-16e (page 101) to make three magnolias pod centers, using 3" of pale green ribbon and 3" of 20-gauge wire. The pod is just like a stemmed berry but slightly elongated.
2. Petals: Use 5" of 1-1/2" wide cream ribbon to make nine inner petals (three for each flower). Use 6" of 2" wide cream ribbon for the 15 outer petals (five for each flower).

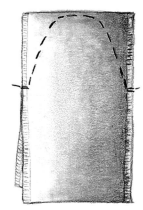

Wild Rose Posy

Make a corsage of wild roses and display them in a crystal vase when not being worn.

I love these roses! You may think these flower colors are too bright but let me tell you, they were inspired by the vintage ones I saw that once graced a 1920's dress. And those were very bright!

These sweet flowers are easy to make and a joy to give. Make bunches of them to share! I am often complimented on the posy when I wear it, and when people find out that it is made of ribbon they are very surprised.

You will need:

27-1/2" peach/cream wire-edge ribbon, 1" wide
13-3/4" peach/apricot wire-edge ribbon, 1" wide
13-3/4" fuchsia/pink wire-edge ribbon, 1" wide
13-3/4" candy pink wire-edge ribbon, 1" wide
13-3/4" hot pink wire-edge ribbon, 1" wide
25" olive green wire-edge ribbon, 1" wide
25" lime green wire-edge ribbon, 1" wide
72" olive green bias-cut silk ribbon, 5/8" wide
18" dark green sheer ribbon, 1" wide
36" of 30-gauge thread-covered wire
60" of 32-gauge thread-covered wire
90 yellow double-headed stamens
12 green double-headed stamens
Tacky glue

Steps:

Make the roses and leaves:

1. Wild roses: Refer to diagrams 31b-31g (page 110) to make six pinch petal roses. Each rose center has 15 double-headed yellow stamens and two green stamens attached to 6" of 30-gauge wire. Refer to diagram 2 (page 96). Make two peach/cream roses, one peach/apricot, one fuchsia/pink, one candy pink, and one hot pink. Each rose has five petals - the back pinched style. Each petal uses 2-3/4" of ribbon. Overlap the petals evenly around the stamens and stitch them in place. Lightly cover the raw edges at the base of the petals with glue and wrap the base with olive green bias-cut silk ribbon and then down the entire wire stem. Cut the excess ribbon and add a touch of glue to the base of the ribbon and wire and roll this in your fingertips to seal the ends.

2. Leaves: Refer to diagrams 37a-37e (page 115) to make ten boat leaves. Make five olive green leaves and five lime green leaves, using 5" of ribbon for each leaf. Stem each leaf with 6" of 32-gauge wire and cover with olive green bias-cut silk ribbon.

Arrange the flowers:

1. Assemble the roses and stemmed leaves in a bunch. Wrap a small piece of wire around the stems to hold the posy together. Cover the wire with an 18" piece of sheer green ribbon tied into a bow.
2. Display the flowers in a perfume bottle, a small silver pitcher, a glass slipper, or have them framed in a deep shadowbox-style frame.

Project Tips

Sew a pin back to the stems or use a corsage pin if wearing the posy.

Techniques Guide

Use this guide as a visual reference to all the ribbonwork techniques found in this book.

On page 118 you will find the **Combination Rose Guide**. This is a summary of how all the combination roses were made. Every time a combination rose is used in a project you will be referred there first so you can identify the rose mentioned. The summary illustrates what techniques to use and indicates where to find the diagrams for those techniques.

Stamens

Diagram 1

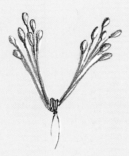

Wrap thread around the center of the stamens. If no stem is required, fold the stamens in half and insert them into the center of a flower.

Diagram 2

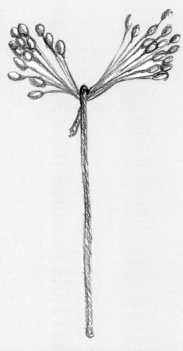

Wrap the stamens with thread and add a wire stem at the center.

Twisting Ribbon

Diagram 3

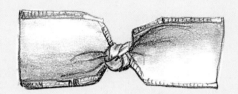

Twist ribbon and stitch to crinoline.

Diagram 3a

Twisted ribbon, stitched in a spiral on crinoline for a flower center. Cut away the excess crinoline.

Knots

Diagram 4

Tie an overhand knot.

Shirring

Diagram 5

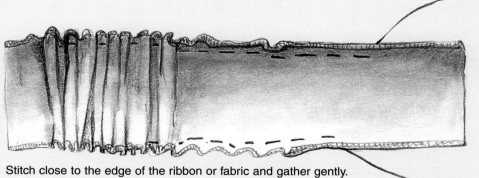

Stitch close to the edge of the ribbon or fabric and gather gently.

Ruching

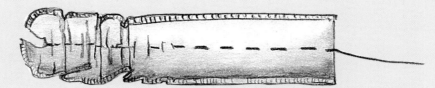

Straight Ruching

Diagram 6

Stitch along the center. Pull the gathering to the desired fullness.

Zigzag Ruching

Diagram 7a

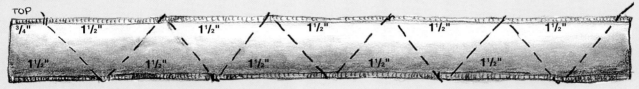

Measure the petal spacing and stitch a zigzag pattern.

Diagram 7b

Gather the ribbon to the desired fullness. If making a flower, gather tightly.

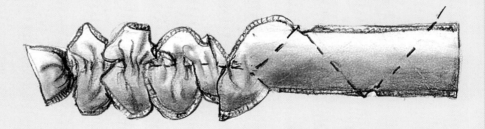

Diagram 7c

If making a flower, trim the excess ribbon under the stitch line.

Diagram 7d

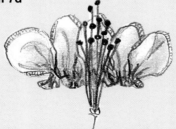

Secure the gathering around the stamens (or in some cases, a coiled rose center).*

Diagram 7e

The finished flower.

Note: When using stamens for the center, insert them before joining the petals together. To flatten the stamen stems in the back of the flower, coil them on themselves and secure with stitches.

Variation 1: Zigzag Ruching With Top Folded Ribbon

Diagram 8

Fold the ribbon in half and press flat. Stitch the pattern. Complete steps 7b through 7d.

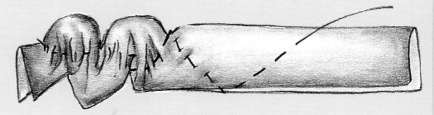

Pleating

Center Pleating

Diagram 9

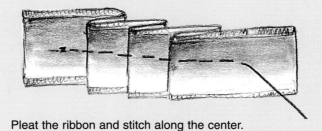

Pleat the ribbon and stitch along the center.

Edge Pleating

Diagram 10

Pleat the ribbon and stitch along the bottom edge. For large ribbons make two rows of stitching along the bottom edge.

Loops

Single Loop Leaf
Diagram 11

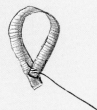

Fold the ribbon and stitch at the base of the loop.

Two Loop Streamer
Diagram 12

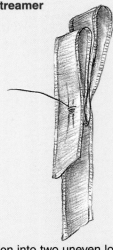

Fold the ribbon into two uneven loops and stitch at the base of the loops.

Three Loop Bow
Diagram 13a

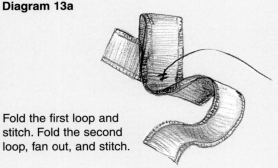

Fold the first loop and stitch. Fold the second loop, fan out, and stitch.

Diagram 13b

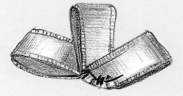

Repeat for the third loop. Fold the excess to the back and trim. Cover the center with a bead.

Five Loop Bow
Diagram 14

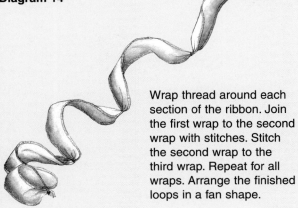

Wrap thread around each section of the ribbon. Join the first wrap to the second wrap with stitches. Stitch the second wrap to the third wrap. Repeat for all wraps. Arrange the finished loops in a fan shape.

Six Loop Flower
Diagram 15

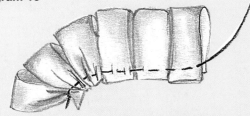

Fold six pieces of ribbon and stitch them together. Gather tightly and secure around a single stamen to form a flower.

Tubes

Berries/Rosehips

Diagram 16a

If the ribbon is wire-edge, remove the top wire. Fold the ribbon in half.

Diagram 16b

Stitch the side seam.

Diagram 16c

Coil the top of the stem wire into a loop. Insert the stem wire. Gather the top of the ribbon tightly, catching the wire loop in the gathering.

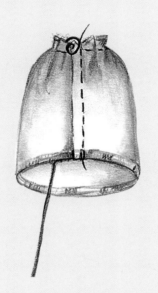

Diagram 16d

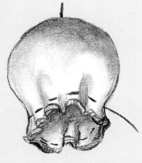

Invert the tube and gently gather near the base edge of the tube.

Diagram 16e

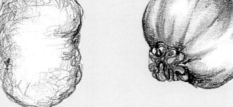

If making a berry, insert a cotton ball and tighten the gathering.

Variation 1: Stem Covers

Diagram 16f

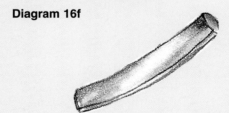

Follow diagrams 16a through 16b. Stitch the long sides of the ribbon. Turn inside out after the seam is stitched.

Variation 2: Bell Flower With Wire-Edge Ribbon

Diagram 16g

Follow diagrams 16a through 16d.

Variation 2: Bell Flower With Ruffle-Edged Ribbon

Diagram 16h

Follow diagrams 16a through 16d.

Variation 3: Bell Flower Made to Lily of the Valley

Diagram 16i

Follow diagrams 16a through 16d.
For a lily of the valley, the opening is pinched closed, not
gathered.

U-Gathers

Single U-Gather

Rosettes and Petals (flat)

Diagram 17a

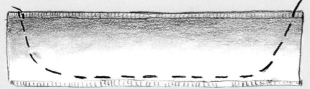

If the ribbon is wire-edge, remove the bottom wire. Stitch the ribbon and gather it to the desired shape. In some cases this gathered ribbon will be simply placed around a rose center rather than being a stand-alone flower.

Large Petal

Diagram 17b

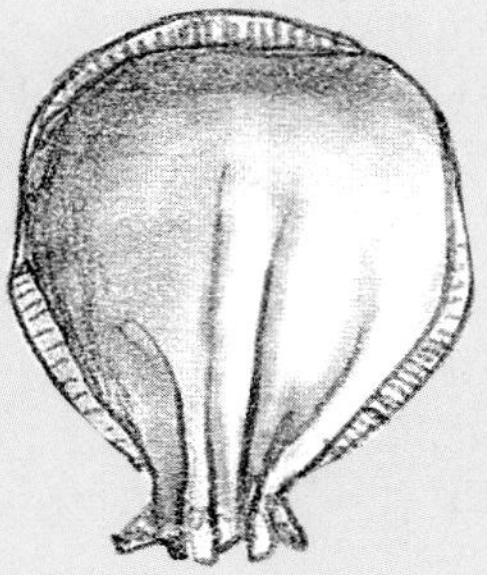

Miniature Petal

Diagram 17c

If making a petal, gather tightly.

Small Basic Rosette

Diagram 17d

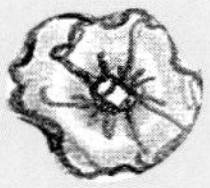

If making a rosette, gather to 1/4", overlap the ends, and stitch them closed. Cover the center with beads.

Larger Silk Ribbon Rosette

Diagram 17e

Double Spiral

Diagram 17f

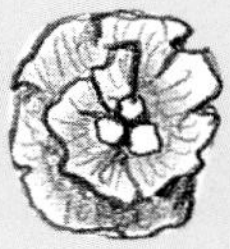

Triple Spiral

Diagram 17g

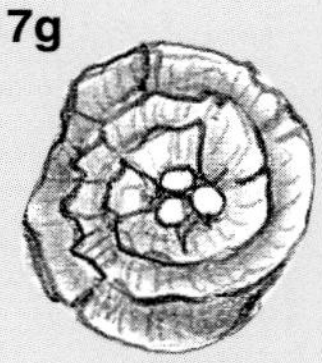

If making a multilayered rosette, stitch one end of the rosette gathering to the center of a small piece of crinoline. Stitch the remaining gathering in a spiral. Cover the center with beads.

Coiled U-Gather (upright)

Diagram 18a

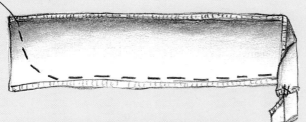

If the ribbon is wire-edge, remove the bottom wire. Stitch the pattern and fold down the right end. Roll the folded end into a cylinder. If the ribbon is too short, skip the stitching and just roll the ribbon up into a cylinder.

Diagram 18b

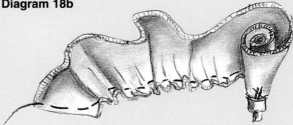

Thread a second needle and secure the base of the cylinder with stitches. Cut the thread. Tighten the gathering and coil around the cylinder.

Diagram 18c

Secure the layers with stitches so the center of the flower doesn't pop out.

Variation 1: Frayed Edge

Diagram 19a

Fray the edge of the bias-cut silk ribbon using your first finger and thumb. Stitch the pattern.

Diagram 19b

Tighten the gathering and coil the ribbon on itself. Secure with stitches.

Variation 2: Bottom Folded Edge

Diagram 20a

Fold the ribbon up by 2/3 or 1/2.

Diagram 20b

Stitch the pattern.

Diagram 20c

Gather to fit the intended use and secure. Separate and fluff the layers of ribbon.

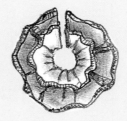

Variation 3: Top Folded Edge

Diagram 21a

Fold the bias-cut silk ribbon in half along its length.

Diagram 21b

Stitch the u-gather with the fold at the top.

Diagram 21c

Gather tightly for a petal.

Diagram 21d

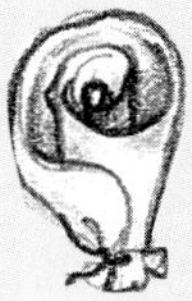

If making a coiled rose center, gather loosely.

Diagram 21e

For a cabochon style rose, arrange three petals around the rose center.

Variation 4: Rolled Edge

Diagram 22a

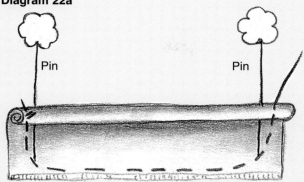

If the ribbon is wire-edge, remove the bottom wire only. Roll the top edge of the ribbon down very tightly, to 2/3 of its original width. For example: 1-1/2" wide ribbon will be rolled down to a 1" width. Stitch the pattern.

Diagram 22b

Gather and secure.

Diagram 22c

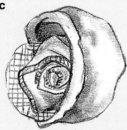

Stitch the petal over the rose center. The petal base and ends are positioned under the crinoline.

Diagram 22d

Finished rose. When stitching the remaining petals over a rose center, overlap them so only one row of petals is formed.

Two-Petal U-Gather

Diagram 23a

If the ribbon is wire-edge, remove the bottom wire. Fold the ribbon into two sections and stitch as shown.

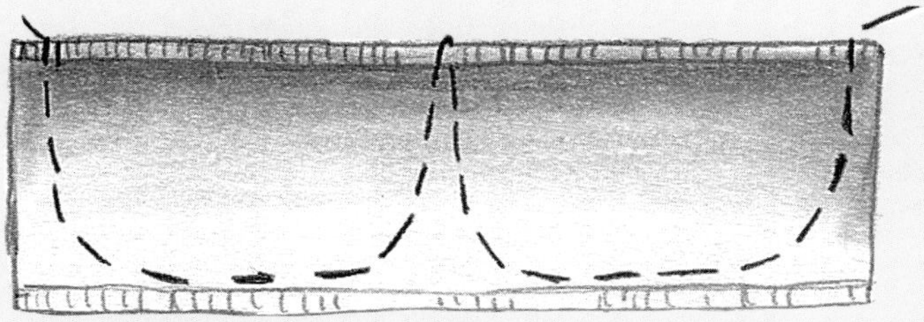

Diagram 23b

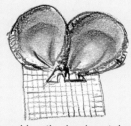

Gather tightly. If making the back petals of a pansy, sew the petals to a small piece of crinoline.

Diagram 23c

Small ruffled-edge ribbon.

Three-Petal U-Gather

Diagram 24a

If the ribbon is wire-edge, remove the bottom wire. Fold the ribbon into three sections and stitch as shown.

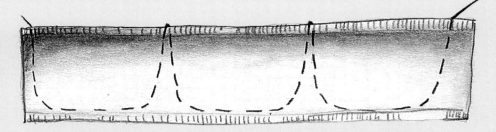

Diagram 24b

Gather to the fullness needed. In some cases these "petals" will go around a flower center. Test the gathering to check the fit and then secure the gathering.

Diagram 24c

If making the front petals of a pansy, gather tightly and stitch to the pansy's back petals.

Four-Petal U-Gather

Diagram 25a

If the ribbon is wire-edge, remove the bottom wire. Fold the ribbon into four sections and stitch as shown.

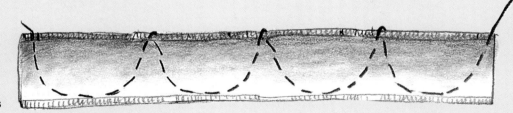

Diagram 25b

If making blossoms, regardless of the ribbon style or size, gather tightly to form four petals. Join the first and last petal together. Note: If using stamens for the center, insert the stamens before joining the petals together. To flatten the stamen stems in the back of the flower, coil them on themselves and secure with stitches. If using beads for the center, add the beads after the petals are joined.

Diagram 25c

Diagram 25d

The flower will look different according to the ribbon used.

Variation 1: Bottom Fold

Diagram 26

Fold the ribbon up 2/3 and stitch the pattern. Gather to the fullness needed to fit around the flower center. Join the petals together after placing them around the flower center. Separate and fluff out the petals.

Five-Petal U-Gather

Diagram 27a

If the ribbon is wire-edge, remove the bottom wire. Fold the ribbon into five sections and stitch as shown. Gather the ribbon.

Diagram 27b

Adjust the gathering around the flower center and secure the gathering. Join the petals. Note: In some cases the petals are stitched and joined together first, and a separate rose center is placed on top of the petals.

Variation 1: Bottom Fold

Diagram 28

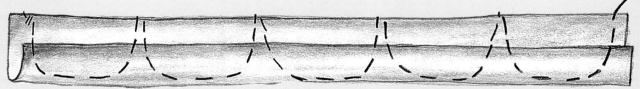

Fold the ribbon up 2/3 and stitch the pattern. Gather to the fullness needed and secure the gathering. Join the petals together after placing them around the flower center. In some cases, a rose center will be stitched on top of the petals.

Petals

Dipped Corner

Diagram 29a

Fold the ribbon in half. Tack both sides of the ribbon, 1/4" down from the fold.

Diagram 29b

Turn the ribbon inside out, keeping the corners tucked in.

Diagram 29c

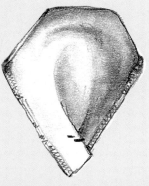

Narrow the bottom of the ribbon with a single pleat. Stitch in place.

Diagram 29d

If the petals are not to be sewn to stamens and stemmed, sew them to a 1/2" circle of crinoline, overlapping them so they fit into one row. Cover the center with rosettes, buttons, larger beads, etc.

Rolled Corner

Diagram 30a

Fold the ribbon in half.

Diagram 30b

Work on the back of the petal first. Fold in one corner.

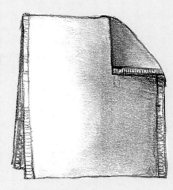

Diagram 30c

Roll this corner again. Secure the roll with a few hidden backstitches from beneath the roll of ribbon. Be careful not to let the stitches show on the front of the petal. Secure the stitches and cut the thread.

Diagram 30d

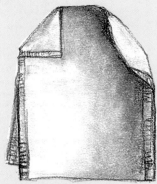

Fold in the other corner.

Diagram 30e

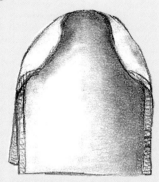

Roll this corner again. Secure the roll with a few hidden backstitches from beneath the roll of ribbon. Cut the thread.

Diagram 30f

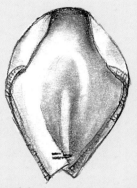

Narrow the bottom of the petal with two pleats. Secure with stitches.

Diagram 30g

Front view of the completed petal.

Diagram 30h

If making a rose that is not stemmed, stitch the first petal to the rose center, keeping the tops of the petals above the top of the rose center. Evenly arrange the remaining petals to fit in the first row.

If making a large rose, stitch the first petal to the rose center, then stitch each consecutive petal to the previous petal, continuing in a clockwise manner until all the petals have been stitched on. The tops of the petals should be positioned slightly higher than the top of the rose center. To secure and tighten the rose, push the needle and thread through all the layers of ribbon near the base of the rose several times. Secure the stitches and trim the excess ribbon from the base.

Pinch Petals

Diagram 31a

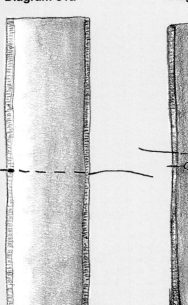

For top pinched petals, stitch across the middle of the ribbon.

Diagram 31b

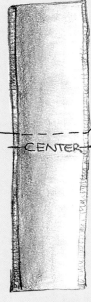

For back pinched petals, mark the ribbon 3/8" from the center of the ribbon and stitch across the ribbon.

Diagram 31c

Gather both styles of petal tightly.

Diagram 31d

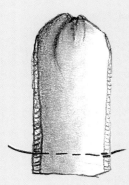

For both styles of petal, fold the ribbon in half. Narrow the base of the ribbon by tightly gathering about 3/16" from the raw edges.

Diagram 31e

Finished front view of top pinched petal.

Diagram 31f

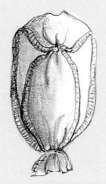

Finished back view of a back pinch petal.

Diagram 31g

Finished Wild Rose with back pinched petals. Note: When using these petals with a stamen center, whether the stamens are on a wire stem or not, stitch the first petal to the stamens, then evenly arrange the remaining petals in a clockwise pattern until one row of petals is formed. They may overlap. If the flower has no stem, coil the stamen ends on themselves in the back of the flower and secure with stitches.

Folded Rose

Diagram 32a

Fold down the right end of the ribbon.

Diagram 32b

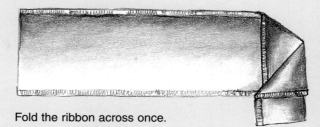

Fold the ribbon across once.

Diagram 32c

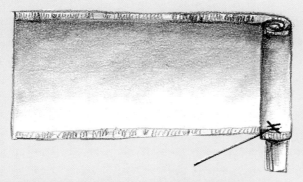

Tightly roll it until the top of the rolled ribbon forms a round cylinder. These rolls are the secret to beautiful rose centers. Stitch the base to secure the ribbon folds. Do not cut the thread.

Diagram 32d

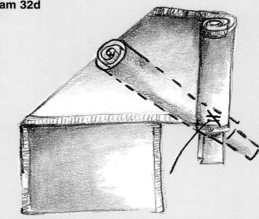

Fold the ribbon on the left toward the back. Tilt the coiled ribbon cylinder (this puts "air" between the folded layers) and roll it across the diagonal fold of ribbon. The top of the cylinder does not rise higher than the folded edge.

Diagram 32e

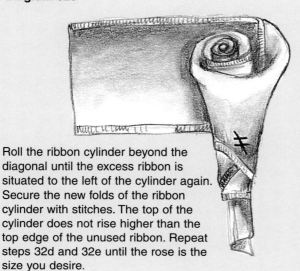

Roll the ribbon cylinder beyond the diagonal until the excess ribbon is situated to the left of the cylinder again. Secure the new folds of the ribbon cylinder with stitches. The top of the cylinder does not rise higher than the top edge of the unused ribbon. Repeat steps 32d and 32e until the rose is the size you desire.

Diagram 32f

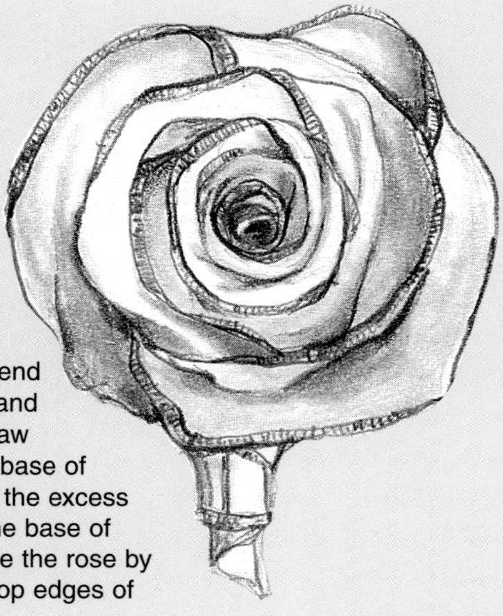

Finish the rose by folding down the last few inches of the end of the ribbon and stitching the raw edge into the base of the rose. Trim the excess ribbon from the base of the rose. Style the rose by pinching the top edges of the ribbon.

Variation 1: Folded Rose With Gathered Extension

Diagram 33

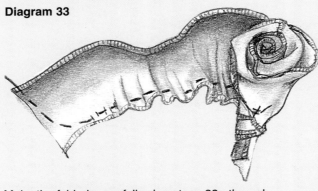

Make the folded rose, following steps 32a through 32e. Depending on the size of ribbon and the amount of gathering needed, gather the remaining length of ribbon and coil the gathering around the folded rose. Secure the coiling with stitches and trim the thread and any excess ribbon from the base of the rose.

Variation 2: Thread Sculpted Folded Rose

Diagram 34a

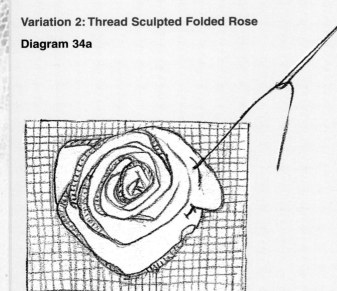

Make the folded rose following steps 32a through 32f. Closely trim the base of the rose and stitch the rose to the crinoline. Begin the "sculpting" by bringing your thread and needle from under the crinoline to the section of the rose ribbon fold you want to shape. Your stitches should be hidden!

Diagram 34b

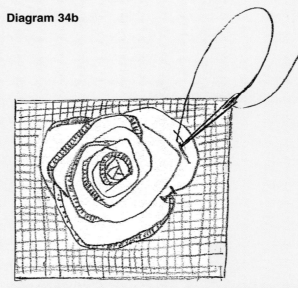

Catch the ribbon with the needle, then bring the needle back down to the underside of the crinoline. Repeat this for all areas of the rose you want to sculpt or shape. If you make a mistake, simply unpick the offending threads and restitch. Don't strive for perfection - no two roses will look the same.

Prairie Point Leaves

Diagram 35a

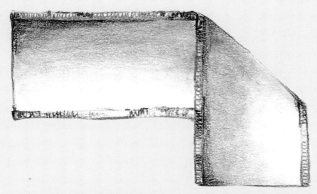

If the ribbon is wire-edge, remove the bottom wire. Mark the halfway point in the ribbon and fold half of the ribbon down.

Diagram 35b

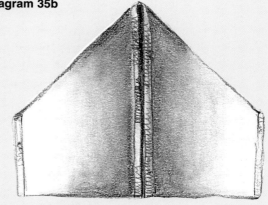

Fold the other half of the ribbon down.

Diagram 35c

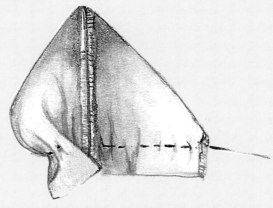

Gather across the bottom, going through all layers of ribbon. Use the bottom of the "triangle" on the back side of the ribbon as a guide to stitch on.

Diagram 35d

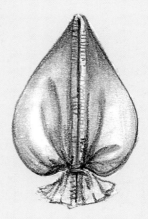

Gather the stitching very tightly, wrap your thread around the base of the leaf once and secure the wrap with a few stitches. Cut the thread and trim the excess ribbon from the base of the leaf.

Curved Leaves

Diagram 36a

If the ribbon is wire-edge, remove the wire along the side that is stitched. Fold the ribbon in half. Stitch the curved pattern shown, starting at the folded end of the ribbon.

Diagram 36b

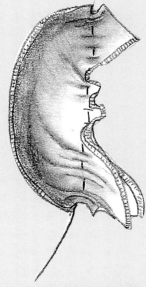

Pull the gathering thread so the side edge is straight.

Diagram 36c

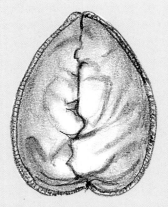

Open the leaf and adjust the gathering to the shape desired. Secure the gathering.

Diagram 36d

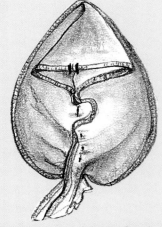

Flatten the tab on the back of the leaf and secure with a stitch.

Boat Leaves

Diagram 37a

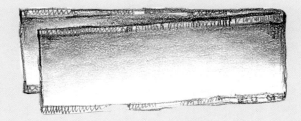

If the ribbon is wire-edge, remove the bottom wire. Fold the ribbon in half.

Diagram 37b

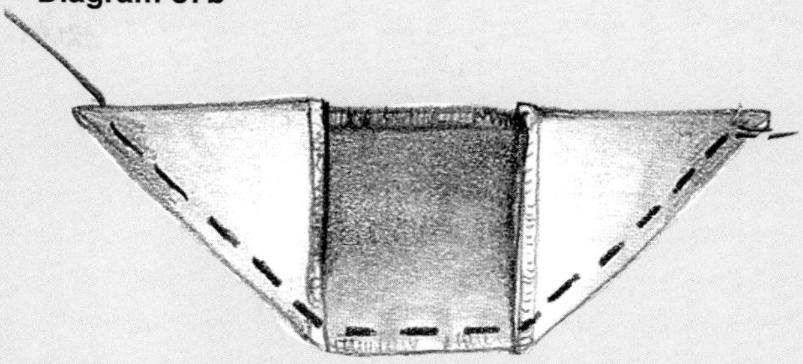

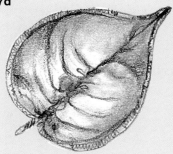

Turn up the bottom corners of the ribbon so a "boat" shape is formed. Begin the stitching pattern from the folded point on the right, continuing along the edge of the ribbon to the other point.

Diagram 37c

Pull the gathering thread so the bottom of the "boat" goes straight.

Diagram 37d

Open the ribbon and test the gathering until the leaf is the shape you want. Secure the gathering with stitches. Trim off the ribbon tabs at the back of the leaf.

Diagram 37e

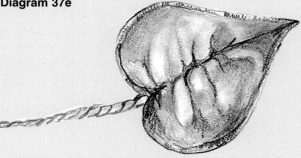

If stemming a leaf, lay the wire on the back of the leaf and whipstitch it to the center of the leaf. Cover the stem wire with bias-cut silk ribbon or floral tape.

Half-Boat Leaf

Diagram 38a

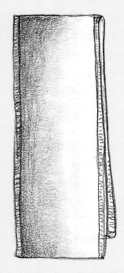

If the ribbon is wire-edge, remove the wire along the side that is stitched. Fold the ribbon in half.

Diagram 38b

Turn down the corner on the folded end of the ribbon and stitch the pattern as shown.

Diagram 38c

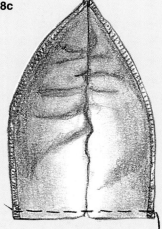

Slightly gather the ribbon, then secure the gathering with backstitches. Open the ribbon and gather across the bottom edge.

Diagram 38d

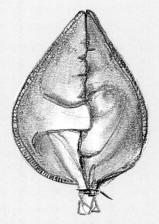

Tightly gather and secure. Trim the tails.

Diagram 38e

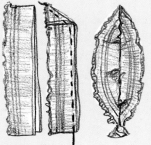

Use narrower ribbons in small compositions.

Mitered Leaves

Diagram 39a

Fold the ribbon in half.

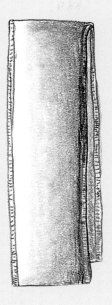

Diagram 39b

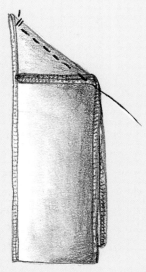

Fold down the corner on the folded edge of the ribbon. Stitch a seam along the diagonal. Secure the stitching and cut off the thread.

Diagram 39c

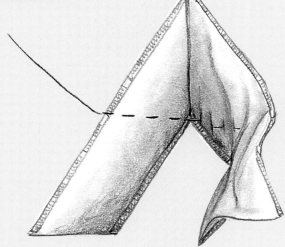

Open the ribbon. Stitch across the ribbon as shown.

Diagram 39d

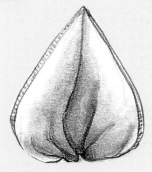

Gather the stitching tightly and secure with backstitches. Trim the ends from the base of the leaf and tuck the tails under. This is an excellent leaf to use if it's openly exposed in a composition with nothing to overlap it.

Combination Rose Guide

A good majority of the roses in this book are made by combining several ribbon techniques. Use this guide as a starting point in learning what comprises a particular rose. An illustration of the rose is listed first, followed by the project name in which it appears. Next is a symbol for the components that make up each rose. Under each symbol is the name of the ribbon technique and a reference to where you will find how to do that technique if you aren't familiar with it.

Name of Rose	*Project Name*	*Start With*	*Add*
 Rose #1	Lady Eleanor, page 34	Folded Rose Diagrams 32a - 32f	Single U-Gather Diagrams 17a, 17d
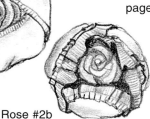 Rose #2a Rose #2b	Peach Brooch, page 41 Dresden Flowers page 22	Folded Rose Diagrams 32a - 32f	Three Single U-Gather Petals Diagrams 17a, 17b
 Rose #3	Black Hat, page 52	Folded Rose Diagrams 32a - 32f	Five Single U-Gather Petals Diagrams 17a, 17b

Name of Rose	*Project Name*	*Start With*	*Add*
 Rose #4	Parasol, page 79	Folded Rose Diagrams 32a - 32f	Two Sets of Three-Petal U-Gathers Diagrams 24a - 24b
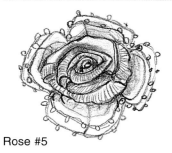 Rose #5	Dresden Flowers, page 22	Folded Rose Diagrams 32a - 32f	 Four-Petal U-Gather, Variation Diagram 26
 Rose #6	Autumn Brooch, page 44	Folded Rose Diagrams 32a - 32f	 Five-Petal U-Gather, Variation Diagram 28
 Rose #7	Parasol, page 79	Folded Rose Diagrams 32a - 32f	Seven Rolled Corner Petals Diagrams 30a - 30h
 Rose #8	Dresden Flowers, page 22	Folded Rose Diagrams 32a - 32f	Five Rolled Corner Petals Diagrams 30a - 30h

Name of Rose	Project Name	Start With	Add

Rose #9

Footstool, page 74

Folded Rose
Diagrams 32a - 32f

Three Rolled Edge U-Gathers
Diagrams 22a - 22d

Rose #10

Dresden Flowers,
page 22

Folded Rose
Diagrams 32a - 32f

Three Single U-Gather Petals
Diagrams 17a, 17b

Five Petal U-Gather
Diagrams 27a-27b

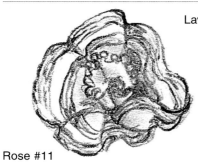

Rose #11

Lavender Sachet,
page 76

Coiled Rose
Diagrams 18a - 18c

Single U-Gather, Variation
Diagrams 20a - 20c

Rose #12

Pink Hat, page 47

Coiled Rose
Diagrams 18a - 18c

11 Rolled Corner Petals
Diagrams 30a - 30h

Name of Rose	*Project Name*	*Start With*	*Add*
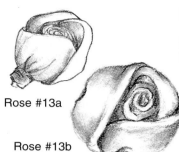 Rose #13a Rose #13b	Brown Brooch, page 38 Ball Gown, page 67 Chatelaine, page 64	Coiled Rose, Variation Diagrams 21a, 21b, 21d	Three Single U-Gathers, Variation Diagrams 21a - 21c
 Rose #14	Chatelaine, page 64	Coiled Rose, Variation Diagrams 21a, 21b, 21d	**A** **B** **A.** Three Single U-Gathers, Variation Diagrams 21a - 21c **B.** Five Single U-Gathers, Variation Diagrams 21a - 21c
 Rose #15	Ball Gown, page 67 Chatelaine, page 64	Coiled Rose, Variation Diagrams 21a, 21b, 21d	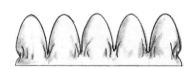 Five-Petal Zigzag Ruching, Variation Diagram 8
 Rose #16	Shoe, page 57	5 Dipped Corner Petals Diagrams 29a - 29d	Single U-Gather Diagrams 17a, 17d
 Rose #17	Peach Brooch, page 41	Twisted Spiral Diagrams 3, 3a	 Five-Petal U-Gather Diagrams 27a, 27b

About the Author

Helen, an Australian now living in the United States, has been involved with crafts and needle arts since 1984. She has demonstrated a wide variety of crafts products for manufacturers at trade shows; has been invited to showcase her creative painting talents for retail companies including Elizabeth Arden cosmetics, and Dillards stores; and she teaches ribbon art to many students throughout the U.S. and Australia. Helen also makes regular appearances on HGTV's Carol Duvall Show with her ribbonwork and half dolls.

Many things inspire Helen - her garden, her antique hat collection, a massive ribbon collection which includes vintage pieces of ribbonwork and a small antique half doll collection. She also enjoys a variety of music and sings with the Rocky Mountain Chorale in Boulder, Colorado.

About the Grant Humphreys Mansion

*T*he house was built in the Beaux-Arts style showcasing a mixture of styles, combining grandiose proportions, detailed terra cotta finishes, balustraded porches and balconies, entablature, and a projecting façade supported by 20-foot columns.

James Benton Grant, the youngest governor of Colorado at 39 years, was the first owner of this mansion. The house was completed in 1902 at a cost of $35,000 and was the scene of many social gatherings among Denver's wealthiest and most powerful families.

In 1917, the widow Grant sold the 30-room mansion to Albert and Alice Boyd Humphreys, well known for successful oil discoveries in Wyoming, Oklahoma, and Texas. The Humphreys family stayed in possession of the house until it was bequeathed to the State of Colorado in 1976. It is now listed on the National Register of Historic Places and has been designated a Denver Landmark.

A mix of vintage ribbon blossoms and a rose on crinoline. Collection of Meron Reinger.

Bibliography

In Style, Jean L. Druesedow, Metropolitan Museum of Art

Ribbon and Fabric Trimmings, Woman's Institute of Domestic Arts and Sciences, Inc., 1925

Ribbon Art, Vol. 1 No. 1, Ribbon Art Publishing Co. Inc., 1923

Ribbon Art, Vol. 1 No. 2, Ribbon Art Publishing Co. of America, Inc.

Ribbon Art, Vol. 1 No. 3, Ribbon Art Publishing Co. of America, Inc.

The Century of Hats, Susie Hopkins, Chartwell Books, 1999

The Collector's Encyclopedia of Half Dolls, Frieda Marion and Norma Werner, Crown Publishers, Inc., 1979

The Half Doll, Shona and Marc Lorrin, Walsworth Publishing Co., 1999

Embossed edges on this British postcard frame a charming maiden with apricot ribbon and carnations in her hair. Circa 1912.

Of interest in this vintage composition of ribbon flowers is the addition of silk chenille thread used to embellish the leaves and flowers. Collection of Meron Reinger.

Resources

Retail

Springwood

1002 Turnberry Circle
Louisville, CO 80027
Web site: www.helengibb.com
E-mail: helen@helengibb.com
Phone: 303-673-0949
Fax: 303-926-0065

Full line of ribbonwork supplies: needles, thread, crinoline, ribbons, ribbon kits, porcelain half dolls, buttons, album kits, laces, and silk prints.

Signed copies of Helen's books, *The Secrets of Fashioning Ribbon Flowers* and *Heirloom Ribbonwork*, are also available. Ribbon retreats, classes, and special tours to Australia are also conducted.

Visit the Web site, call, or write for the latest information. Send a SASE #10 envelope (and $3 if requesting a product brochure. Refundable with first order).

The Ribbon Club

PO Box 699
Oregon House, CA 95962
Web site: www.theribbonclub.com
Phone: 530-692-3014

A club for ribbon lovers. Subscribe to the Flower and Seasonal ribbon collections. A great way to build a ribbon collection!

Artemis, Inc.

179 High St.
South Portland, ME 04106
Web site: www.artemisinc.com
Phone: 888-233-5187

The largest online and mail order source for the famous Hanah Silk bias-cut silk ribbons.

Wholesale

Renaissance Ribbons
PO Box 699
Oregon House, CA 95962
Web site: www.renaissanceribbons.com
Phone: 530-692-0842
Fax: 530-692-0915

Mokuba
55 West 39th St.
New York, NY 10018
Phone: 212-869-8900
Fax: 212-869-8970

A fantastic red bow crowns this straw hat. Artist, Aveline. Austrian Postcard, 1919.

Index

Album, embellished, 72
Ball gown, embellished, 67
Basket, embellished, 19, 22
Beading, in project, 15, 42, 45, 63, 66, 77
Bell flower
    in project, 81
    technique, 102
Berries
    in project, 39, 92
    technique, 101
Blossoms
    in project, 45, 53, 58, 62, 75, 78
    ruched, in project, 39
Boué Soeurs, 68, 69
Bow, in project, 29, 51, 56, 58, 75
Box, embellished, 8, 14, 16, 25
Brooch, 38, 41, 44
Button
    antique, 17, 18, 42
    knob, 21
Chatelaine, 31, 64
Cocarde, in project, 48-49
Corsage, 94
Daffodil, 85, 88, 89
Dandelion, in project, 51
Fan, in project, 59
Feather, in project, 53
Footstool, embellished, 74
Forget-me-nots, in project, 51
Glue, 12
Gown, embellished, 67, 68-69
Grant Humphreys Mansion, 123
Half doll, 57
    dress, 27, 30, 35
    history, 29
    project, 25, 28, 32, 34
Hat
    embellished, 46-56
    needle case, 54
Hatpin holder, 57
Hydrangea, in project, 81
Jonquil, 85, 86
Kaufman Millinery, 53
Knot, technique, 96
Knot flower, in project, 29
Leaves
    boat

    in project, 23, 43, 81, 95
    technique, 115
  curved
    in project, 33, 35, 40, 51
    technique, 114
  half-boat
    in project, 15, 20, 26, 40, 43, 62, 66, 70, 75
    technique, 116
  loop, in project, 29
  mitered
    in project, 23, 45, 59, 75, 81
    technique, 117
  prairie point
    in project, 15, 23, 43, 45, 51, 56, 58, 81
    technique, 113
Lily of the valley
    in project, 42
    technique, 102
Loop
    in project, 23, 56, 83
    technique, 100
Lord and Taylor, 4
Lorrin, Shona and Marc, 29
Magnolia, 92
Milliner, The, 46, 51
Needle book, 31
Needle case, 54
Pansy, in project, 29, 81
Parasol, 79
Petal, technique, 108-110
Petunias, in project, 51
Pincushion, 28, 54
Pleating, technique, 99
Posy, 94
Purse, 61
Ribbon, purchasing, 12
Ribbon, twisting, technique, 97
Ribbon Art, 9
Ribbon Book, The, 9
Rose
  cabochon, in project, 75
  coiled, in project, 15, 29, 56, 81
  combination
    in project, 23, 35, 39, 42, 45, 49, 53, 58, 65-66, 69-70, 75, 78, 81

The novelty "people" bookmarks shown above and on page 128 are made of ribbon and are French, circa 1920s. Collection of Deborah Piefke.

technique, 118-121
folded
   in project, 15, 20, 23, 29, 33, 35,
      51, 56, 58, 70, 78, 81, 83
   technique, 111-112
pinch petal
   in project, 81, 95
   technique, 110
tea rose, in project, 49, 81
Rosebud, in project, 23, 42, 65, 75
Rosehip
   in project, 45
   technique, 101
Rosette
   in project, 20, 23, 26, 33, 39, 43, 58,
      62, 66, 70, 75, 78
   technique, 103
Ruching, technique, 98
Ruffle, in project, 40
Sachet, 34, 76
Scarf chatelaine, 64
Shirring, technique, 97
Shoe, 57
Silk print, 15
Stamen
   in project, 86, 88, 89, 90
   technique, 96
Stem tube cover
   in project, 87, 88, 91
   technique, 101
Stitch length, 12
Stitching, 12
Supplies, 11
Sweet pea, in project, 42
Tassel, 32, 77
Tea bag pouch, 18
Tea caddy, 16
Tubes, technique, 101
Tulip, 85, 90
U-gather, technique, 103-107
   bottom folded edge, 104
   coiled, 103
   five-petal, 107
   four-petal, 106
   frayed edge, 104
   rolled edge, 105
   single, 103
   three-petal, 106
   top folded edge, 104
   two-petal, 105

More Fabulous Heirloom Ideas From Helen Gibb

THE SECRETS OF FASHIONING
Ribbon Flowers
HEIRLOOMS FOR THE NEXT GENERATION

by Helen Gibb

What to do with all that gorgeous ribbon available today? Easy, fashion the most elegant flowers imaginable. Incorporate 15 different flowers, roses, pansies, violets, sweet peas, carnations, peonies, to name a few, into jewelry, home decor, wearables, and more. Also included are instructions for making the leaves, calyx, and stems.

Softcover • 8-1/4 x 10-7/8 • 128 pages
150 b&w Illustrations • 100 color photos
Item# FFFGD • $24.95

The Art of Ribbonwork

*R*ibbonwork, an age-old form of surface embellishment, is enjoying a wonderful revival today. With the myriad of exquisite ribbons now available, combined with the instructions found in this book, you will soon be creating beautiful flowers, bows and trims to embellish dresses, hats, purses and boxes - heirlooms for the next generation.

In this lavishly photographed book, ribbon expert Helen Gibb brings her passion for heirloom ribbonwork to you in the form of 27 elegant projects that include half-doll pincushions and tassels, brooches, albums, boxes and much more. All are easily made by following the clear instructions for each project and by learning the ribbonwork techniques found in the illustrated step-by-step Techniques Guide and the wonderfully simple Combination Rose Guide.

> "Helen transforms beautiful ribbons into exquisite creations and her artistry is enviable. But when her teaching makes her art accessible to the rest of us, she becomes truly inspirational!"
>
> *Monique, The Ribbon Club*

> "Creativity, generosity, enthusiasm, and patience are qualities I look for in a teacher. Helen Gibb is, without a doubt, one of a select group of teachers I have encountered who possesses those qualities in abundance."
>
> *Linda Stimson, student from California*

> "Helen's detailed teaching style takes the mystery out of ribbonwork techniques that may otherwise seem too complex for many of us to learn. She always inspires the creativity that is innate in each of us."
>
> *Vicki Jones, student*

Helen Gibb, television personality and author of the best-selling book, *The Secrets of Fashioning Ribbon Flowers*, has been involved with crafts and needle arts since 1984. She has been invited to showcase her creative painting talents for retail companies including Elizabeth Arden cosmetics and Dillards stores, and she teaches ribbon art to many students throughout the U.S. and Australia. Helen also makes regular appearances on HGTV's "Carol Duvall Show" with her ribbonwork and half dolls.

ISBN 0-87341-991-X $24.95